Modern Critical Interpretations

William Shakespeare's
Much Ado about Nothing

Modern Critical Interpretations

These and other titles in preparation

Modern Critical Interpretations

William Shakespeare's
Much Ado about Nothing

Edited and with an introduction by
Harold Bloom
Sterling Professor of the Humanities
Yale University

Chelsea House Publishers ◊ *1988*
NEW YORK ◊ NEW HAVEN ◊ PHILADELPHIA

© 1988 by Chelsea House Publishers,
a division of Chelsea House Educational Communications, Inc.

Introduction © 1988 by Harold Bloom

Printed and bound in the United States of America

10 9 8 7 6 5 4 3 2 1

∞ The paper used in this publication meets the minimum requirements of the American National Standard for Permanence of Paper for Printed Library Materials, Z39.48-1984.

Library of Congress Cataloging-in-Publication Data
William Shakespeare's Much ado about nothing.
  (Modern critical interpretations)
  Bibliography: p.
  Includes index.
  1. Shakespeare, William, 1564–1616. Much ado about
nothing. I. Bloom, Harold. II. Series.
PR2828.W55 1988   822.3′3   87-25590
ISBN 0-87754-934-6 (alk. paper)

Contents

Editor's Note

This book brings together a representative selection of the best modern critical interpretations of Shakespeare's comedy *Much Ado about Nothing*. The critical essays are reprinted here in the chronological order of their original publication. I am grateful to Cornelia Pearsall for her erudite aid in editing this volume.

My introduction reflects briefly upon the mutually strong nihilism that underlies the wit of Beatrice and Benedick. Ruth Nevo begins the chronological sequence of criticism with an admirable analysis of Benedick and Beatrice as "heretics and mockers." Sexual politics is the subject of Harry Berger, Jr.'s characteristically brilliant essay, which suggests that "Hero seems both to admire and envy Beatrice and to disapprove of her."

John Traugott studies *Much Ado about Nothing* as a drama of mixed genre combining comedy with romance, a contamination that can control and rationalize fantasy. Centering upon Claudio, Joseph Westlund isolates the lover's self-fulfilling paranoia and fear of manipulation. In Richard A. Levin's reading, the play is a study in barely hidden hostilities and consequent aggressivities.

The dark vision of marriage, prevalent throughout the Shakespearean wisdom, is illuminated in *Much Ado* by Carol Thomas Neely, who shows that the play indeed has affinities both with "festive comedies" and with "problem comedies." Karen Newman concludes this volume by tracing the tragicomic pattern that links *Much Ado* to *Measure for Measure*.

Introduction

A. P. Rossiter found the essence of the Beatrice-Benedick relationship in misprision or mutual misreading by those two fierce wits:

> Benedick and Beatrice misapprehend both each other *and* themselves: each misprizes the other sex, and misapprehends the possibility of a complete agreement between them, as individuals, on what causes that misprision: love of freedom and a superior conceit of themselves as "wise" where others are fools; as "free" and untied; and as having a right to enjoy kicking over other people's traces.

That is an interestingly dark view of Beatrice and Benedick, and is akin to Harold Goddard's judgment when he wrote of "antiromantic and intellectual egotism in Beatrice and Benedick" as being an aspect of the "egotism of youth." Both Rossiter and Goddard were among the double handful of critics who stood out among earlier modern Shakespearean expositors, but I have never been easy with the stance either adopted towards Beatrice and Benedick. Why moralize in regard to this couple, of all couples? Do they not represent, in *Much Ado about Nothing*, a freedom that misinterprets precisely because it *is* the freedom to misinterpret? And is such freedom, as represented by them, merely a youthful egotism?

If these questions are answerable, then it may be that the answers turn upon change, and the representation of change, in Beatrice and Benedick. Comedy is, of course, a much more difficult genre in which to depict change than is tragedy or history, but one of Shakespeare's uncanniest gifts was to abolish genre, and not just in what we have agreed to call his "problem plays." Here are Beatrice and Benedick in their full splendor:

1

BENEDICK: Thou and I are too wise to woo peaceably.
BEATRICE: It appears not in this confession; there's not one
  wise man among twenty that will praise himself.
BENEDICK: An old, an old instance, Beatrice, that liv'd in the
  time of good neighbors. If a man do not erect in this
  age his own tomb ere he dies, he shall live no longer
  in monument than the bell rings and the widow weeps.
BEATRICE: And how long is that, think you?
BENEDICK: Question: why, an hour in clamor and a quarter
  in rheum; therefore is it most expedient for the wise,
  if Don Worm (his conscience) find no impediment to
  the contrary, to be the trumpet of his own virtues,
  as I am to myself.

Do they misinterpret one another or themselves? We must acknowledge that, like all great wits, they are self-conscious and self-
congratulatory, failings (if those are failings) present also in Falstaff,
Rosalind, and Hamlet. I think that *Much Ado about Nothing* generates
its highest humor, properly performed, precisely because Beatrice and
Benedick understand their rituals all too well. Nor will age wither
their youthful egotism; mutually supportive, it will last out their lives
together. Shakespeare represents them as changing, but only into stronger
versions of their initial selves. Anne Barton usefully compares them to
Katherina and Petruchio in *The Taming of the Shrew*, another "uncon-
ventional couple who arrive at love and understanding by way of
insult and aggression." Her characterization is closer to those earlier
lovers than to Beatrice and Benedick, who understand (and probably
love) one another from the start or even before the start.

Rossiter thought that *Much Ado about Nothing* was "a fantasy of
equivocal appearances in a glittering world of amiable fools of all
sorts." It is certainly the most amiably nihilistic play ever written,
and is most appositely titled. Beatrice and Benedick are Nietzscheans
before Nietzsche, just as they are Congreveans before Congreve.
The abyss glitters in every exchange between the fencing lovers,
whose mutual wit does not so much defend against other selves as it
defends against meaninglessness. You make much ado about nothing
because nothing will come of nothing. Emersonians also before
Emerson, Beatrice and Benedick confront and pass the pragmatic
test, the experiential law of Compensation, that nothing is got for
nothing. When they totally accept that, the play can end, because

by then they have changed altogether into the strongest version of their own selves:

BENEDICK: Do not you love me?
BEATRICE: Why, no, no more than reason.
BENEDICK: Why then your uncle and the Prince and Claudio
    Have been deceived. They swore you did.
BEATRICE: Do not you love me?
BENEDICK: Troth, no, no more than reason.
BEATRICE: Why then my cousin, Margaret, and Ursula
    Are much deceiv'd, for they did swear you did.
BENEDICK: They swore that you were almost sick for me.
BEATRICE: They swore that you were well-nigh dead for me.
BENEDICK: 'Tis no such matter. Then you do not love me?
BEATRICE: No, truly, but in friendly recompense.
LEONATO: Come, cousin, I am sure you love this gentleman.
CLAUDIO: And I'll be sworn upon't that he loves her,
    For here's a paper written in his hand,
    A halting sonnet of his own pure brain,
    Fashion'd to Beatrice.
HERO: And here's another
    Writ in my cousin's hand, stol'n from her pocket,
    Containing her affection unto Benedick.
BENEDICK: A miracle! here's our own hands against our
    hearts. Come, I will have thee, but by this light, I take
    thee for pity.
BEATRICE: I would not deny you, but by this good day, I
    yield upon great persuasion, and partly to save your
    life, for I was told you were in a consumption.
[BENEDICK]: Peace, I will stop your mouth.
                               [*Kissing her.*]

"Better Than Reportingly"

Ruth Nevo

Much Ado about Nothing contrasts notably with the early *Shrew*, which is similarly structured in terms of antithetical couples, not only in its greater elegance of composition and expression, but in its placing of the comic initiative in the hands of its vivacious heroine Beatrice. In both plays, as indeed in all of the comedies, courtly love conventions and natural passion, affection and spontaneity, romance and realism, or style and substance, saying and believing, simulation and dissimulation interlock; while the dual or agonistic structure of courtship allows for reversals, exchanges and chiastic repositionings of those contraries during the dynamic progress of the plots. In *Much Ado,* moreover, Shakespeare modifies his usual multiple-plot practice. He normally has a sub- or midplot which functions as a distorting mirror for the main plot, exaggerating to a degree of positive aberration the deficiencies adumbrated in the latter, while the lower-order fools provide at once a ridiculing parody of the middle characters and a foil for the higher recognitions of the higher ones. As Salingar points out, "it appears to be necessary for the lovers to act out their fantasies, and to meet living images or parodies of themselves before they can rid themselves of their affectations and impulsive mistakes." Here, however, as in *The Shrew,* it is at first blush hard to tell which is model and which parody. Beatrice and Benedick's unorthodox views on marriage are a parody of normal conventions and so confirm Hero and Claudio in their soberer ways. Only later do we perceive that it is the conventionality, and

From *Comic Transformations in Shakespeare.* © 1980 by Ruth Nevo. Methuen, 1980.

subsequent frailty, of the Hero/Claudio relationship that provides a flattering reflector for the freewheeling, impulsive, individualist demands of Beatrice and Benedick.

That it is the authenticity of the subplot Beatrice-Benedick relationship which is finally paramount is vouched for by the response of audiences. From its earliest appearances the play was received as the story of Beatrice and Benedick—Charles I himself is a royal witness. But this again does not do justice to the whole. D. P. Young would have us "stop speaking of plot and sub-plot in Shakespearean comedy" altogether, finding the "uniqueness of the form" in the mirroring of themes in all the strands of action. But it is the specific equilibrium of the two plots in *Much Ado,* with Hero and Claudio remaining insistently, and not only formally, the official main protagonists, and Beatrice and Benedick challenging their monopoly of attention, which buttresses our perception of the dialectic of contraries the play embodies. As Alexander Leggatt has skillfully argued, in opposition to those who tend to ignore Hero and Claudio, or to find them insipid or pasteboard figures:

> The love affair of Beatrice and Benedick, so naturalistically conceived, so determined by individual character, is seen, at bottom, as a matter of convention. In praising its psychological reality we should not overlook how much the pleasure it gives depends on the essential, impersonal rhythm it shares with the other story.

Benedick and Beatrice are the latest in a line of heretics and mockers and the most complex. In the earlier comedies the lover is perceived as the absurd and predictable victim of his love-longing and his lady's imperious aloofness, and is mocked by impudent individualists like Speed and Moth. Shakespeare's dialogue with the courtly lover has advanced in stages, and by the constant locating and relocating of couples in dynamic opposition to each other. In *The Comedy of Errors* it is the Antipholus twins who are opposing doubles: one the worried, married man—a realist; the other the ardent and idealistic courtly lover. In *The Shrew* there is a neat reversal of oppositions which foreshadows *Much Ado*: the antiromantic couple find love-in-marriage, the apparently ardent lovers find cold comfort in theirs. In *The Two Gentlemen* doubles appear again, more complexly, in Valentine the devoted ex-heretic, and Proteus the treacherous ex-votary of courtly love. The deadlocking of these extremities is resolved only by the substantial presence of the loving Julia. In *Love's Labour's Lost* all the men—initially heretics—become courtly-love romantics, while all the women play the role of satirical realists. Berowne, who mocks love, both style and substance, becomes an advocate and acolyte of the very *dolce stil nuovo* he formerly disdained. But he can still be fooled by a reliance on rhetoric which lacks real substance, as Rosaline points out. The conventions and the substance of courtly love are turned upside down for the doubled couples in *A Midsummer Night's Dream,* but balance is restored through the "cure" of the married lovers. Anne Page and Fenton, those honest bourgeois lovers, have no romantic style, overshadowed as they are by the matrimonial problems of the stout matrons of Windsor; but they sensibly make off, leaving their worthy parents to patch up their marriages as best they may. Now Benedick and Beatrice, forewarned apparently, disavow love, placing no faith in its conventional vows and protestations, but are very much affected by the substance of the passion; while for Claudio and the compliant Hero the courtly love conventions camouflage a courtship of convenience, the substance of which will be tested and found wanting. Further turns are to come. Rosalind, deeper in love than there are fathoms to measure it, becomes a pert Moth herself, mocks her sonneteer lover, and exposes the conventional style of the quasi-courtly lovers Phebe and Silvius as very cold Pastoral and quite empty of substance; while Orsino, the very impersonation of the courtly-love style, is liberated from its insubstantiality by the substantial discovery of a girl in his personable young page's clothes. And there the dialectic rests, a romantic heroine having been created whose various follies, acted out, prove transcendently beneficial, and whose self-assured wit can contain even what Leggatt calls "the comically unoriginal situation of being in love."

What is wanting at the outset of *Much Ado* is a match for Claudio, and a match for the high-spirited Lady Beatrice—the two "matches" are poised against each other in double antithesis. Claudio, back from the wars and eager to "drive liking to the name of love," replies gratefully and decorously to the Duke's offer of intercession:

> How sweetly you do minister to love,
> That know love's grief by his complexion!
> (1.1.312–13)

But already in act 1, scene 1, Claudio's "Hath Leonato any son, my Lord?" alerts us to the substance behind the rhetoric of "Can the world buy such a jewel?" "Seven hundred pounds, and possibilities, is a goot gift" as Evans sensibly put it in *The Merry Wives*. Matchmaking is afoot and Claudio has a weather eye for material circumstances. "Love's griefs, and passions" are perfunctory, the accepted, conventional, romantic rhetoric which masks a relation essentially impersonal. Claudio is asking "Who is Hero, what is she?" but his enquiries it will be noticed, are about others' opinions of her, with which to endorse her value for him. And the Prince's agreement to act proxy suitor for him is both further endorsement that the match is desirable, and further indication of the absence of need on Claudio's part for the direct challenges and intimacies of courtship. He does, when he feels himself cheated, bitterly exclaim:

> Therefore all hearts in love use their own tongues.
> Let every eye negotiate for itself,
> And trust no agent; for beauty is a witch
> Against whose charms faith melteth into blood.
>
> (2.1.177–80)

But his eye is on the treachery of the proxy suitor, not on the object of his attentions.

Nothing could be more appropriate than that such a relationship should be vulnerable to the slightest breath of scandal. Nor that in the church scene Claudio should utter the contemptuous

> There, Leonato, take her back again.
> Give not this rotten orange to your friend.
>
> (4.1.31–32)

He is accusing a business associate of bad faith in the conveyance of shoddy goods, and blatantly violating all accepted convention to do so. But he also thereby gives expression to the animosity latent behind the chivalric mask. Poor Hero faints away under the shock, as well she might. For this is her world upside down—a nightmare of hostility, a midsummer night's dream without benefit of magic, and a revelation of the hollowness and inauthenticity of their relationship.

The match has been counterfeit; its romantic rhetoric camouflage for purely practical proprieties and proprietorships; and it is consonant with the exquisite symmetry of this play that Claudio's second wedding, formally reversing the ill effects of the first, is with an anonymous and unknown—a camouflaged—bride. It is her anonymity, however, that turns out to be, mercifully, counterfeit. Unreconstructed aggressiveness has been exorcized in the church scene and the ritual expiation makes possible a second chance.

Against this pair, stand Beatrice and Benedick. These would-be lords and owners of their faces are sturdily nonconformist. "I had rather hear my dog bark at a crow than a man swear he loves me" (1.1.131–32). Thus Beatrice, and Benedick is of a similar mind: "God keep your ladyship still in that mind! so some gentleman or other shall scape a predestinate scratched face" (1.1.133–35). Benedick is a professed tyrant to the opposite sex, an "obstinate heretic in the despite of beauty" (1.1.234–35), and Beatrice, too, a confirmed "batchelor":

> For hear me, Hero: wooing, wedding, and repenting, is as a Scotch jig, a measure, and a cinquepace; the first suit is hot and hasty, like a Scotch jig, and full as fantastical; the wedding, mannerly-modest, as a measure, full of state and ancientry; and then comes repentance, and with his bad legs falls into the cinquepace faster and faster, till he sink into his grave.
>
> (2.1.72–80)

In these two hostility is not latent but flagrantly proclaimed. They give each other no quarter in the merry war. Benedick is a braggart, a stuffed man, little wiser than a horse, as fickle as fashion itself, caught like a disease, the prince's jester, a dull fool; it is a dear happiness to women that he loves none. Beatrice is Lady Disdain, Lady Tongue, a parrot teacher, a chatterer, a harpy; he will go to the world's end rather than hold three words with her. However, though they maintain loudly that they cannot stand each other it does not require superhuman powers of perception to observe the marked interest, little short of obsession, they take in each other.

It is no other than Signior Mountanto that Beatrice enquires about, and no other than Beatrice who occurs to Benedick as the model with which to compare Hero, to the latter's disadvantage: "There's her cousin, and she were not possess'd with a fury, exceeds her as much in beauty as the first of May doth the last of December" (1.1.190–92). Their antiromantic posture is therefore also a mask, as has frequently been noted, aggressive-defensive and designed to forestall the very pain it inflicts. For example, "I wonder that you will still be talking, Signior Benedick, nobody marks you" (1.1.116–17), is an interesting opening ploy. It translates into a whole set of messages. First of all, someone does. She does. Clearly she has, provocatively, caught his attention, when (we infer) he was ostentatiously *not* marking her. Then, I wish no one *did* mark you, you great fool, *not* being marked being the greatest punishment possible to a boaster like yourself, and therefore a good revenge. Revenge for what? Not for your not having marked me, certainly. Don't imagine that I mark you, or that you are the least important to me, or that I in the least care whether you mark, marked, or will mark me. "What, my dear Lady Disdain! Are you yet living?" (1.1.118–19). And they are off.

What came between these two in the past is half concealed and half revealed. One infers a quarrel: "In our last conflict four of his five wits went halting off, and now is the whole man govern'd with one; so that if he have wit enough to keep himself warm, let him bear it for a difference between himself and his horse" (1.1.65–70). One infers a roving eye on Benedick's part: "He set up his bills here in Messina and challeng'd Cupid at the flight" (1.1.39–40) and "He wears his faith but as the fashion of his hat: it ever changes with the next block" (1.1.75–77). Later, we hear explicitly: "Indeed, my lord, he lent it [his heart] me awhile, and I gave him use for it, a double heart for his single one. Marry, once before he won it of me with false dice, therefore your Grace may well say I have lost it" (2.1.278–82).

Benedick's protestations too, partly conventionalized caution against cuckoldry, smack of the once bitten, who now demonstratively projects an image of invulnerability: "Prove that ever I lose more blood with love than I will get again with drinking, pick out mine eyes with a ballad-maker's pen, and hang me up at the door of a brothel-house for the sign of blind Cupid" (1.1.250–54). "Alas, poor hurt fowl! Now will he creep into sedges" (2.1.202–3), says Benedick of Claudio, whose proxy wooer has stolen his girl, it seems; and immediately reverts to his own affront: "But that my Lady Beatrice should know me, and not know me!" (2.1.203–4). A similar image appears again, significantly, just before the gulling of Beatrice:

> For look where Beatrice like a lapwing runs
> Close by the ground, to hear our conference.
>
> (3.1.24–25)

One infers wounded susceptibilities on both sides and one therefore perceives that where Claudio's idealization of love-and-marriage is the packaging he and his milieu regard as suitable for an eminently practical and profitable marriage arrangement, these others deidealize love and marriage as an insurance against a recurrence of loss.

At the masked ball the comic disposition of Messina is paradigmatically dramatized. Hearsay and conjecture dominate. That the Prince woos for himself is assumed by all, and how can one know with so much rumour about? The point about the limitations of knowledge and the tendency to jump to conclusions is made graphically by the masked ball itself. Pedro and Hero evidently recognize each other. Margaret and Balthasar (possibly) don't; Ursula knows Antonio, whom she recognized by the wagging of his head and whom she flatters upon his excellent wit, though he swears he counterfeits. What of Beatrice and Benedick? Who is pretending? Does Benedick, recognizing her, take the opportunity of a gibe about her having her wit out of the *Hundred Merry Tales*? Does Beatrice, as he evidently believes, not recognize him and therefore speak from the heart when she calls him "the Prince's jester"? Or is this taunt her knowing revenge for Benedick's gibe about the *Hundred Merry Tales*? Which possibility is confirmed by Benedick's soliloquy after the ball: "But that my Lady Beatrice should know me, and not know me"? Does he mean at the ball specifically, or in general? Is he angry at not being recognized, or at not being appreciated? These two take particular pride in their wit, it will be noticed, and no affront will be less easily forgiven than disparagement on that score. Whether both now assume that the other really means the wounding things he or she says, or both know that the other was intentionally meaning to wound, a new turn is giving to the warfare between them. We no longer witness the reflection of an old quarrel but the quick of a new one. There is no reason, however, why the spiral should ever stop since the dynamics of self-defence will ensure that the more they pretend to ignore each other the more they will fail, *and* the more wounded their self-esteem will become. It is a knot too hard for them to untie, but fortunately there are plotters at hand.

The comic disposition of Messina is thus to be taken in: to dissimulate, or simulate, to be deceived by appearance, or by rumors. The sophisticates go further. They do not believe what they really want to believe, or do believe what they perversely do not want to believe. "I should think this a gull, but that the white-bearded fellow speaks it. Knavery cannot sure hide himself in such reverence" (2.3.118–20). Or, for that matter, they believe what they really do not want to believe, like Leonato, who says in the church scene

Would the two princes lie, and Claudio lie,
Who lov'd her so, that speaking of her foulness,

Wash'd it with tears?
(4.1.152–54)

It is, indeed, precisely the last of the logical possibilities that the remedy in this play must bring about, causing both couples, reassured, really to believe what they really want to believe without recourse to defence or counterdefence maskings.

Even the good Dogberry masks his ineptitude with liberal borrowings from the learned languages but—a tertiary irony—when he most desires that Borachio's aspersion of assdom be recorded, so that the mockery of the law it implies be made public, all that he succeeds in making public is the open and palpable truth of the aspersion. Masking in this play is a fertile generator of dialectical ironies.

Only Don John, who despises "flattering honest men," cannot hide what he is. He would rather "be disdain'd of all than to fashion a carriage to rob love from any," and boasts of not wearing a mask—he is a plain-dealing villain, he says. But this is *his* illusion, of course, since in his plot to defame Hero he does precisely "fashion a carriage," and it is only that sharp lot, the constabulary, who capture the deformed thief Fashion wearing "a key in his ear and a lock hanging by it" (5.1.308–9)—a piece of creatively significant nonsense—that save the day.

The comic device—both eavesdropping tricks—ironically both deception and source of truth, is perfectly adapted to mesh with, exacerbate and finally exorcize this comic disposition. One eavesdropping strategem is benignly plotted by the well-meaning Duke who aims to bring Signior Benedick and the Lady Beatrice into a mountain of affection "th' one with th' other," the other malignly staged by Don John who aims to cross the marriage his brother has arranged; and both are marvellously counterpointed by the inadvertent overhearings of those stalwart guardians of the law and the city—Dogberry's watch. It is worth noticing that when the first plot of Don John fails he at once sets about devising another, any marriage his legitimate brother arranges being grist to his mill; and the failed plot at the masked ball deftly gives us advance notice of the play's modalities of masking and mistaking, of tests and testimonies.

Don Pedro's plot provides the plotters with the opportunity to tease their victims with some home-truths real or imagined. On the men's side:

DON PEDRO: She doth well. If she should make tender of her
love, 'tis very possible he'll scorn it, for the man (as
you know all) hath a contemptible spirit.

CLAUDIO: He is a very proper man.

DON PEDRO: He hath indeed a good outward happiness.

CLAUDIO: Before God, and in my mind, very wise.

DON PEDRO: He doth indeed show some sparks that are like
wit.

CLAUDIO: And I take him to be valiant.

DON PEDRO: As Hector, I assure you, and in the managing
of quarrels you may say he is wise, for either he avoids
them with great discretion, or undertakes them with a
most Christian-like fear.

(2.3.178–90)

And the women's:

HERO: But nature never fram'd a woman's heart
Of prouder stuff than that of Beatrice.
Disdain and scorn ride sparkling in her eyes,
Misprising what they look on, and her wit
Values itself so highly that to her
All matter else seems weak. She cannot love,
Nor take no shape nor project of affection,
She is so self-endeared.

(3.1.49–56)

But the cream of the jest in the eavesdropping scenes is that those who
speak the truth believe that they are inventing it.

Beatrice and Benedick are thus equivocally provided with apparently "objective" testimony concerning the real state of the other's
affections, and the defensive strategy each adopted becomes supererog-
atory. Benedick, abandoning his armour, contrives to preserve some
semblance of a complacent self-image:

Happy are they that hear their detractions, and can put them
to mending. . . . I may chance have some odd quirks and
remnants of wit broken on me, because I have rail'd so long
against marriage; but doth not the appetite alter? A man
loves the meat in his youth that he cannot endure in his age.
Shall quips and sentences and these paper bullets of the
brain awe a man from the career of his humor? No, the

world must be peopled. When I said I would die a bachelor,
I did not think I should live till I were married.

(2.3.229–44)

But Beatrice abandons hers with an immediate generous contrition:

Can this be true?
Stand I condemn'd for pride and scorn so much?
Contempt, farewell, and maiden pride, adieu!
No glory lives behind the back of such.
And, Benedick, love on, I will requite thee,
Taming my wild heart to thy loving hand.

(3.1.107–12)

Whether Beatrice and Benedick were hiding their real selves until
reassurances of reciprocity overcame psychological barriers, or whether
they were caused to suffer love by the magic of knowing themselves
recipients of affection, they both abandon themselves to the fantasy of
love. Their status, however, as objects of comic mockery is skilfully
preserved by the necessary time lag of the contrivance. When Benedick
is convinced that he is loved while Beatrice is still her old self, the folly
of rationalization displays itself at large before our very eyes. Benedick's
response to Beatrice's as yet untransformed scorn is ingenuity itself, at
work upon most unpromising material:

Ha! "Against my will I am sent to bid you come in to
dinner"—there's a double meaning in that. "I took no more
pains for those thanks than you took pains to thank me"
—that's as much as to say, "Any pains that I take for you is
as easy as thanks."

(2.3.257–62)

And when each in his or her transformed state—transformed be it
noted into the very style of suffering love they originally ridiculed—
when each meets his or her friends, each undergoes the teasing equivalent of the scorn they once poured upon lovers, and survives!

The benignly staged eavesdropping releases undissimulated feeling
in Beatrice and Benedick by apparently disclosing the feelings of the other.
It is paralleled by the malignly staged eavesdropping, which apparently
exposes Hero to Claudio by its sham disclosure of her dissimulation,
and releases the passion in which Claudio will destroy (temporarily)
his own happiness, and a lovely lady, in the church "unmasking."

The point I wish to emphasize is the consummate realization of the Shakespearean comic therapy which these symmetries produce. Both plottings bring out, in diametrically opposed ways, the implications of the protagonists' masks; both trigger an acting out of what was hidden and latent: the joyous dream of love proved and requited—a homeopathic *remedia amoris*—in the case of Beatrice and Benedick; a nightmare fantasia of enmity in the case of Claudio and Hero.

Don John, says Anne Barton, "a plot mechanism more than a complex character in his own right, appears in the play as a kind of anticomic force, the official enemy of all happy endings." It is a striking insight, for it is not by chance that the malign plotter sets off a malign, potentially tragic dialectic of either/or, while the benign plotter releases a benign dialectic of both/and—the comic resolving principle itself. *Much Ado* achieves what the double plot of *The Merchant* fails to achieve: exorcism without a scapegoat, and comic metamorphoses in which the fooled outwit, in their folly, the wisdom of the foolers.

In addition to the admirable ordering of affairs in the higher stratum of society the burlesque eavesdropping of the watch is a tour de force of comic subplot strategy. Unstaged and inadvertent, it discloses counterfeit and exposes truth without the vessels of this providential occurrence having for one moment the dimmest conception of what is afoot. It is therefore ironic foil to the benign fooling of the good plotters and their victims who do know, at least partly, what they are about, and ironic parody of the folly of the malignant plotters and theirs.

Dogberry's anxiety to be star performer at the enquiry occurs just as Leonato is hurrying off to the wedding and cannot, understandably, take the time clearly required to get to the bottom of Dogberry's dream.

> A good old man, sir, he will be talking; as they say "When the age is in, the wit is out." God help us, it is a world to see! Well said, i'faith, neighbor Verges. Well, God's a good man; and two men ride of a horse, one must ride behind. An honest soul, i'faith, sir, by my troth he is, as ever broke bread; but God is to be worshipp'd; all men are not alike, alas, good neighbor!
>
> (3.5.33–40)

This anxiety culminates only in disappointment at not having been written down an ass, but he does succeed in exposing the crafty Borachio and Conrade for the wrongdoers they are.

Dogberry's comic hybris or "delusion of vanity," his blithe confidence in the "gifts that God gives," thus mocks that of all his betters. He is the fulcrum upon which the wit-folly dialectic turns, in a riot of ironic misprisions. He is also the cause of the play's double peripeteia: the climactic church scene, which he could have prevented, and the confession of Borachio, which he nearly does prevent. This double peripeteia marks the final exhaustion of the comic device. Both plots, the benign and the malevolent, have succeeded. Beatrice and Benedick have been tricked into love, Claudio and Hero tricked out of it. The apparently deceitful Hero is unmasked, and this precipitates the unmasking to each other of Beatrice and Benedick, each knowing the other indirectly, by hearsay, rumour and opinion, and only presently to know each other through direct confrontation.

When they reveal themselves to each other, Benedick boldly and Beatrice now hesitant, their knowledge is unmediated either by others, or by their own self-induced obliquities. Now they will really believe what they really want to believe, and have in practice already believed "better than reportingly." But the repudiation of Hero presents them with a further acid test. It is a test of trust, which is as different from belief as knowledge from opinion. "Kill Claudio" is Beatrice's demand that he trust absolutely her absolute trust in her cousin's innocence. It is a dangerous moment. Beatrice plays for high stakes—her lover for her cousin. And if he agrees he will wager beloved against friend. It is the moment of incipient disaster for which the fortunes of comedy produce providential remedies—in this case the voice of that sterling citizen, Dogberry, uncovering the thief Fashion—"flat burglary as ever was committed"—in the next scene. Beatrice puts the reluctant Benedick to the oldest of chivalric tests—to kill the monster and rescue the lady, thus proving his valour and his love. It is a fantasy of knight errantry, and his commitment to this mission, in response to her fierceness, transforms the whole flimsy romance convention into the deadly seriousness of his challenge to Claudio. This is a reversal of all expectations and roundly turns the tables upon the tricksters.

Beatrice's violence is more than passionate loyalty to her cousin. In the war of the sexes with Benedick, Beatrice's combativeness is self-defence, self-assertion, the armour of a vulnerable pride. But when she says "Would it not grieve a woman to be overmaster'd with a piece of valiant dust? to make an account of her life to a cold of wayward marl?" (2.1.60–63); or replies to Pedro's "Will you have me lady?" with "No, my lord, unless I might have another for working-days. Your Grace is too costly to wear every day" (2.1.327–29), we are invited to perceive an added ingredient. She will not have a husband with a beard, or without one; she will not have a husband at all. St Peter will show her where the bachelors sit in heaven and there "live we as merry as the day is long." She will be no meek daughter like her cousin: "But yet for all that, cousin, let him be a handsome fellow, or else make another cur'sy, and say, 'Father, as it please me' " (2.1.53–56). She will be won on her own terms or not at all.

It is a grave demand for independence she is making; and it is possible to infer from her mockery of Benedick's soldiership and from the significant touch of envy in the remark, "he hath every month a new sworn brother" (1.1.72–73), that it is at the circumscription of her feminine condition as much as anything that the Lady Beatrice chafes. She suffers, as we are to discover, love. But before she is love's sufferer she is love's suffragette. And when she says with passion

> you dare easier be friends with me than fight with mine enemy . . . O that I were a man . . . O God, that I were a man! I would eat his heart in the market place . . . or that I had any friend would be a man for my sake . . . I cannot be a man with wishing; therefore I will die a woman with grieving.
>
> (4.1.298–323 passim)

she is far from the acceptance of biological fact. And so Benedick's acceptance of her challenge, in love, and in trust, and in identification with her point of view, proves the very safety valve Beatrice's accumulated truculence requires. In *As You Like It* there is a reverse, though precisely equivalent moment when Rosalind faints at Oliver's story of Orlando's rescue and wounding, and the episode serves quite clearly as a safety valve for Rosalind's hidden and temporary stifled femininity. There, too, the episode marks the exhaustion of the device (the disguise) and precipitates recognitions.

What *Much Ado* invites us to understand about its comic remedies is only fully articulated by the end of the dénouement. Act 5 has to do with question of the visible and the invisible, the seen and the unseen, upon which trust ultimately depends. There is no need for trust if all is open and palpable. Since, in human affairs, nothing is ever open and palpable, much ado about nothing or "noting" ensues. By noting of the lady, says the Friar

> I have mark'd
> A thousand blushing apparitions
> To start into her face, a thousand innocent shames
> In angel whiteness beat away those blushes,
> And in her eye there hath appear'd a fire
> To burn the errors that these princes hold
> Against her maiden truth
>
> (4.1.158–64)

and his proposal is to allow time and the rehabilitating "study of imagination" to bring

> every lovely organ of her life
> Shall come apparell'd in more precious habit,
> More moving, delicate, and full of life,
> Into the eye and prospect of his soul
>
> (4.1.226–29)

while Hero herself, given out as dead, be concealed from sight.

The theme is plentifully embodied in act 5. First in the further glimpse of the incipient tragic possibilities; the father's grief, which he refuses to hide, the young men's self-righteous callous arrogance. This is followed by the appearance of a Benedick, outwardly unchanged, inwardly transformed, outdaring his friend's baiting concerning "Benedick the married man." Finally, taking in that Benedick is in "most profound earnest" for, Claudio is sure, the love of Beatrice, Don Pedro's contemptuous dismissal: "What a pretty thing man is when he goes in his doublet and hose and leaves off his wit!" (5.1. 199–200). This immediately precedes Dogberry's entrance with the bound Borachio and the revealed truth. Borachio rubs it in: "What your wisdoms could not discover, these shallow fools have brought to light—" (5.1.232–34) but no new pieties about "what men daily do, not knowing what they do," will bring Hero back. Claudio must clear his moral debt and he must be seen to do so. It is fitting that he do this by placing himself totally in Leonato's hands:

> O noble sir!
> Your overkindness doth wring tears from me.
> I do embrace your offer, and dispose
> For henceforth of poor Claudio.
>
> (5.1.292–95)

It is himself that he surrenders to Leonato and to his masked bride. And while Claudio thus places himself in trust with Leonato, Beatrice and Benedick flaunt their hidden trust with an outward show of their old defensive combativeness, and a mock denial, till their own letters give them away, of the love we have heard them confess.

> BENEDICK: Come, I will have thee, but, by this light, I take
>   thee for pity.
> BEATRICE: I would not deny you, but, by this good day,
>   I yield upon great persuasion, and partly to save your
>   life, for I was told you were in a consumption.
>
>   (5.4.92–96)

The masked wedding neatly symbolizes the antinomies of seeing and knowing. Benedick's kiss stops not only Beatrice's mouth, but the seesaw of hearsay and double talk, of convention and counterconvention.

The taming of Beatrice has been a more formidable undertaking than that of Katherina because she supplies more varied and imaginative occasions for the comic pleasure wit provides; and with no remedy will we be satisfied that denies us these. If humour and vivacity, individuality, resilience, spontaneity, fantasy and irony are to be the price of wedding bells, no marriage Komos will seem to us a celebration. But the beauty of it is that comedy's double indemnity is triumphantly validated in the final teasing. We are to have our self-assertive witty cake and eat it, too, *con amore*; the remedy—this imagined possibility of remedy—for that suffering state not being such as to deprive us of the value of Beatrice's and Benedick's wit once its function as protective mask is rendered unnecessary. Head and heart, style and substance, convention and nature, are for once—man being a giddy thing—in consonance.

But if the battle of the sexes has thus been won to the satisfaction of both parties, as is comically proper, it is still, in *Much Ado*, by means of a heroine only half divested of her traditional feminine garb. Even "Kill Claudio" is a command which reflects the immemorial dependence of lady upon knight, and, as we have seen, the lady Beatrice chafes at it. The next step, however, is presently to be made, in *As You Like It*, which also harks back to an earlier play. And just as the comparison between *Much Ado* and *The Shrew* (or *Love's Labour's Lost*) provided a measure not only of the scope and subtlety of Shakespeare's growing art but of the changes in its nature, so does comparison between the page disguise of the forlorn Julia and that of Rosalind.

Against the Sink-a-pace: Sexual and Family Politics in *Much Ado about Nothing*

Harry Berger, Jr.

> For, hear me, Hero: wooing, wedding, and repenting is as a
> Scotch jig, a measure, and a cinquepace: the first suit is hot
> and hasty like a Scotch jig (and full as fantastical); the
> wedding, mannerly modest, as a measure, full of state and
> ancientry; and then comes Repentance and with his bad legs
> falls into the cinquepace faster and faster till he sink into his
> grave.
>
> *(Much Ado about Nothing 2.1.63ff.)*

"Sink-a-pace" is the way Sir Toby Belch pronounces the name of the
five-step dance, and I borrow his pronunciation here because it signi-
fies a slowing-down that beats against the galliard tempo of the dance.
In Beatrice's formula, marriage, the afterlife of the wedding, is re-
named repentance, and its tempo is divided into the two mutually
intensifying rhythms suggested by placing Toby's pronunciation in
tandem with Beatrice's description: on the one hand, the decelerating
sink-a-pace of the yoke of boredom, the long dull anticlimax to the
fantastical jig and stately measure; on the other hand, the frenetic
reaction in which the penitent tries ever more desperately and vainly to
escape back into jigtime, tries to make himself giddy with acceleration
and spin himself into forgetfulness. The state and ancientry of the
wedding indicate the influence of the older generation, the father's
interest in and control of the alliance that seals his daughter's future.

From *Shakespeare Quarterly* 33, no. 3 (Autumn 1982). © 1982 by The Folger
Shakespeare Library.

Since Repentance is male, the bad-legged dancer may suggest either the husband himself or else the dominant tone which he—the dominant partner—gives to the monogamous relationship he finds himself unnaturally confined in by what Gloucester, in *King Lear,* called "the order of law."

Beatrice begins her little lecture with "here me, Hero," and it is difficult, on hearing the ear pun, not to add it to the senses of her name. Most of the "noting" about which there is much ado consists of hearing or overhearing. Hero, who says almost nothing in the first two acts, hears a great deal, probably more than what is good for her. If she notes what we note, she hears enough to make her feel that her fate in life is to be her father's passport to self-perpetuation, a commodity in the alliance market, the spoils of the love wars—inevitably a conquered Hero, "overmastered with a piece of valiant dust" who guarantees her anonymity by giving her his name and making her the prisoner and trophy that validates the name. Hero's name threatens to be her fate: Mrs. Hero. Yet even this most male-dominated of heroines betrays more than once her sense of her complicity in the sexual politics of Messina.

The first clue to this sense appears in the brief dance scene beginning at 2.1.75. When Hero responds to the masked Don Pedro's request for a promenade, the conditions she imposes sound like a self-description: "So you walk softly and look sweetly and say nothing, I am yours for the walk," (2.1.76–77). It is as if she is quite conscious of the principle of behavior to which she conforms, and in offering her role to the Prince she may, by a mere shift of the shifters, indicate the value and objective of that behavior: "So long as I walk softly and look sweetly and say nothing, I am yours for the walk," and for the sink-a-pace as well. During all but one (l. 32) of the first 141 lines of the play she had looked on sweetly and silently, saying nothing while her cousin Beatrice crossed swords with Benedick and the other men, and saying nothing while her father entertained a vapid joke or two about her legitimacy and his own easy assurance that he is no cuckold. "Is this your daughter?" Pedro asks:

> LEONATO: Her mother hath many times told me so.
> BENEDICK: Were you in doubt, sir, that you asked her?
> LEONATO: Signior Benedick, no; for then you were a child.
> (1.1.94–96)

And Pedro, after a gibe at Benedick, graciously responds that "the lady fathers herself. Be happy, lady for you are like an honorable father" (1.1.98–99). Benedick will not leave this alone: "If Signior Leonato be her father, she would not have his head on her shoulders for all Messina, as like him as she is" (1.1.100–2). Bizarre as that image is—Hero wearing her father's bearded and graying head as a mask or visored helmet—it may have some truth as an emblem.

After 1.1.32, Hero is silent until 2.1.5, where all she can summon up is one softly and sweetly limping line in support of Beatrice's comment that Don John's sour looks give her heartburn: "He is of a very melancholy disposition" (2.1.5). It is therefore a pleasant surprise to hear an unexpected surge of spirit in her dialogue with the Prince at the masked ball. Remember the situation: the Prince had offered to woo her for Claudio but had been wrongly overheard by her Uncle Antonio's man, who thought Pedro wanted her for himself. As a result, Leonato decided to break the good news to her so "that she may be the better prepared for an answer." Thus when the visored prince says, "Lady, will you walk about with your friend," she seems to know who her friend is, and has her answer ready:

> HERO: So you walk softly and look sweetly and say nothing,
>   I am yours for the walk; and especially when I walk
>   away.
> PEDRO: With me in your company?
> HERO: I may say so when I please.
> PEDRO: And when please you to say so?
> HERO: When I like your favor, for God defend the lute
>   should be like the case!
>
> (2.1.76–83)

Hero peels off her mask of soft, sweet silence and becomes frisky. She tries to flirt, then to banter like Beatrice, and we suddenly see why the Prince's bastard brother has called her "a very forward March-chick" (1.3.49). Her carrying-on keeps the Prince from getting to the point—telling her he is Claudio—before they move out of earshot. He has to coach her in the art: "speak low if you speak love" (2.1.87)—"not so loud, not so fast, let's go off by ourselves and be serious." Since he does not know that she expects his proposal (so that if he pretends to be Claudio she will think it really is the Prince pretending to be Claudio), and since these are the last words we hear, even the audience is not entirely sure of what happens until over a hundred lines later. When

Hero next comes on stage, at 2.1.190, it is in time to hear herself compared to a stolen bird's nest being returned to its owner, and to be traded to Claudio by her father as part of a package deal that includes Leonato's fortunes. She seems easily to reconcile herself both to the match and to the role of commodity, but I think we are allowed at least a momentary doubt as to whether she and Leonato would not have preferred the Prince to Claudio, especially when she hears the Prince casually offer himself to Beatrice after giving Claudio back his bird's nest.

Even if we do not seriously entertain this doubt, we cannot help noticing something else about these scenes, namely that Hero's silence is the correlative of Beatrice's witty noise. Beatrice hogs the stage, and does not let Hero and Claudio savor their betrothal by basking in the limelight; she manages the scene, gives them their cues, gets the affair quickly settled, and then, pushing it aside with "Good Lord, for alliance" (2.1.285), redirects attention to herself and her brief flirtation with the Prince. It is not only that the absence of parents seems to give her a freedom Hero might well envy: since no honorable father's head burdens her shoulders, she can father herself and fight men with their own weapons. It is also that in Hero's presence she continually puts down the norms Hero is trained to respect and the institutional functions Hero is destined to fulfill.

What I find most interesting about all this is that Hero seems both to admire and envy Beatrice and to disapprove of her. This is suggested in her responses to the masked Prince. Her pert "I may say so when I please" (2.1.80) reflects a struggle between two contrary pieces of advice she had just heard: on the one hand, Leonato warning Beatrice that "thou wilt never get thee a husband if thou be so shrewd of tongue" (2.1.16–17) and Antonio counseling Hero to be ruled by her father (2.1.43–44); on the other hand, Beatrice countering Antonio's advice with "Yes, faith. It is my cousin's duty to make cursy and say, 'Father, as it please you.' But yet for all that, cousin, let him be a handsome fellow, or else make another cursy, and say, 'Father, as it please me' " (2.1.45–46). Hero follows with an attempt to masquerade briefly as Beatrice while respecting her filial obligation. If we agree with the Pelican editor that she is flaunting "her permission to say 'yes,' " then her "when I please" takes on a cutting edge, since it means "when my father lets me." Her effort to say "as it please me" and emulate Beatrice fails in the utterance and turns instead into an implicit rejection of Beatrice's rebellious attitude.

If Hero's behavior during the rest of the play lends support to these narrowly based interpretive remarks, then she is a much more interesting character than she has been made out to be, for she not only reflects the limitations of her culture but also betrays a dim awareness of them. This comes out more clearly in her behavior during the gulling of Beatrice. She tells Ursula that when Beatrice hides to over-hear them

> Our talk must only be of Benedick.
> When I do name him, let it be thy part
> To praise him more than ever man did merit.
> My talk to thee must be how Benedick
> Is sick in love with Beatrice. Of this matter
> Is little Cupid's crafty arrow made,
> That only wounds by hearsay.
>
> (3.1.17–23)

Their parts had obviously been assigned by Don Pedro, the Cupid who devised these crafty practices, and to whom Hero had promised— with a fine concern for both her own image and the smooth function-ing of society—that she would "do any modest office . . . to help my cousin to a good husband" (2.1.334).

Though she goes into the scene with an altruistic motive, helping soon turns into hunting. With Ursula she eagerly takes up Cupid's arrow, birdbolt, and fishhook, and marches into ambush, impatient to see the golden Beatrice-fish "greedily devour the treacherous bait" (3.1.28), the "false sweet bait that we lay for it" (3.1.33). But the bait turns out to be neither false nor sweet, and Hero makes sure the hook of love is sharp, so that when the wounded Beatrice swallows the bait she will also swallow her pride. Hero's reciting her part in the Prince's script—she is to speak of Benedick's love-sickness—only prepares us to see how far she strays from it. For she is herself a weapon of the Prince, and of her father, and of the Men's Club of Messina, and what she wants to harp on is Beatrice's disdain. The vigor with which she berates her cousin suggests that she is doing more than pretending for Beatrice's benefit. She only pretends to pretend; the game of make-believe is a self-justifying blind, an altruistic mask, from behind which she can stalk Beatrice with "honest slanders" (3.1.84), letting her know what she really thinks of her, what she really feels, without (for once) being interrupted or put down:

> Disdain and scorn ride sparkling in her eyes,
> Misprizing what they look on; and her wit
> Values itself so highly that to her
> All matter else seems weak. She cannot love,
> Nor take no shape nor project of affection,
> She is so self-endeared.
>
> (3.1.51–56)

The implied contrast is of course to her own quiet, reliable, unappreci-
ated girlscout self. Unlike herself, Beatrice "never gives to truth and
virtue that / Which simpleness and merit purchaseth" (3.1.69–70).

> No, not to be so odd, and from fashions,
> As Beatrice is, cannot be commendable.
> But who dare tell her so? If I should speak,
> She would mock me into air; O, she would laugh me
> Out of myself, press me to death with wit.
>
> (3.1.72–76)

Hero thinks it wrong to rebel against fathers and husbands. The
world must be peopled, and it is disconcerting to be told that marriage
is virtue's repentance rather than its reward. Yet something more than
her own wounded pride comes through in the language she uses to
humble her cousin. There is a touch not only of envy but of grudging
admiration in such images as the fish with golden oars cutting the
silver stream, and the haggards of the rock whose spirits are "coy and
wild" (3.1.35). And consider the following passage, in which Shakespeare oddly allows the usually quiet Hero to break into epic simile: she
tells Ursula to bid Beatrice

> steal into the pleachèd bower,
> Where honeysuckles, ripened by the sun,
> Forbid the sun to enter—like favorites,
> Made proud by princes, that advance their pride
> Against that power that bred it.
>
> (3.1.7–11)

This is a displaced analysis of the whole situation, as well as a figura-
tive embodiment of Hero's complex attitude. Beatrice is the rebellious
favorite advancing her virgin pride against the masculine forces that
ripen it—the solar energy of parents, princes, and admirers. But com-
parisons are odorous, and the simile does not quite work the way Hero

wants it to: the courtly figure strains against the positive quality of its floral subject.

It seems natural, lovely, and even fulfilling for honeysuckle to transform the sun's pride and power into its own, to ripen a fragrant shade, make an enclosed garden where women might protect themselves from princely or paternal penetration. What the imagery implies about Hero is that although she criticizes Beatrice's rebellious pride and independence, she finds them attractive and could even, perhaps, wish for the spirit to photosynthesize her own disdain. With the scorn sparkling in her eyes, Beatrice models an enviable alternative that calls into question Hero's pliant submission to the sun. According to the logic of her image, the alternative chosen by Hero is not pollination but pruning: to be married is to have womanhood's natural ripening into freedom interrupted by the wrench that will reduce her to a sprig worn by some conquering hero. Thus by putting down Beatrice and helping her to a husband, Hero will either eliminate the shadow cast over her own self-effacing commitment, or else she will triumph over Beatrice by reducing her to her own level—that is, by condemning her into everlasting redemption.

Beatrice's view of marriage as a sink-a-pace of repentance is by no means exceptional in *Much Ado about Nothing*. Benedick seems to share it:

> Is't come to this? In faith, hath not the world one man but he will wear his cap with suspicion? Shall I never see a bachelor of threescore again? . . . An thou wilt needs thrust thy neck into a yoke, wear the print of it and sigh away Sundays.
>
> (1.1.175–79)

Don John agrees: "What is he for a fool that betroths himself to unquietness?" (1.3.41). It is conventional male wisdom that women are not to be trusted: "O, my Lord, wisdom and blood combating in so tender a body, we have ten proofs to one that blood hath the victory" (2.3.154–56). Leonato says this for the benefit of the listening Benedick, but as his response to his daughter's defamation later shows, that is no indication that he does not accredit its truth. The ease, indeed the alacrity, with which Leonato, Claudio, and the Prince seize on Hero's guilt confirms what they already suspect, and what they seem happy to suspect. It validates the conventional wisdom, and it affords them the added pleasure of having their sense of merit injured.

It is difficult, however, to reconcile the opinion that men are more sinned against than sinning with another which seems to have equal weight:

> Sigh no more, ladies, sigh no more!
>   Men were deceivers ever,
> One foot in sea, and one on shore;
>   To one thing constant never.
>   Then sigh not so,
>   But let them go,
>   And be you blithe and bonny,
> Converting all your sounds of woe
>   Into Hey nonny nonny.
>
> (2.3.59–67)

The Prince acclaims this as "a good song" (2.3.73), and I think his behavior throughout the play shows that although in this instance he may be referring to the music, in general he agrees with the sentiment. However playfully, he treats courtship as a military campaign, or a hunt, or a set of behind-the-back maneuvers—*practices,* as he calls them. He promises Claudio to take Hero's "hearing prisoner with the force / And strong encounter of my amorous tale" (1.3.292–93); like a good engineer and physician, he will bridge the flood of Claudio's passion, and fit his disease with a remedy (1.1.284–93). Since as Benedick concludes, "man is a giddy thing" (5.4.106), men as well as women can be tricked into giving up their avowed and natural resistance to love and marriage. And in fact, not only *can* they be so deceived; they *must* be, for they would never march off willingly to what both know is a prison that constrains all their natural urges.

The difference between men and women in this respect—so goes the regnant ideology of the play—is that women are responsible for their sins but men are not. Male deception and inconstancy are gifts that God gives, and their proper name is Manhood. But woman has an awesome responsibility. Since she bears her father's fame and fortune into the future as if—to borrow Benedick's image—she wore his head on her shoulders, and since by marrying she assumes the management not only of her husband's household but also of his reputation and honor, she is expected to conquer blood with wisdom even though the odds are ten to one against it. It may be that men dislike the virtue they both praise and lay siege to: they seem to demand the perfections of Diana only in order to prove that Diana, like Astraea, fled the earth long ago, in the time of good neighbors, leaving it to the corruptions of Venus. Claudio's bitter but obvious satisfaction in being victimized owes partly to the fact that it reaffirms his moral superiority: "as a brother to a sister," he whines, I "showed / Bashful sincerity and comely love" (4.1.51–52), while you,

> You seem to me as Dian in her orb,
> As chaste as is the bud ere it be blown;
> But you are more intemperate in your blood
> Than Venus, or those pamp'red animals
> That rage in savage sensuality.
>
> (4.1.55–59)

A virgin who under false pretenses seeks associate membership in the Men's Club of Messina deserves whatever sentence she receives.

On the other hand, the song tells the members of the club that "the fraud of men was ever so, / Since summer first was leavy" (2.3. 70–71). Men are born deceivers whose nature is to be inconstant, untrustworthy, lustful, contentious, and obsessed with honor, status, and fortune. This enables them to think better of themselves, and worse of women. Not only can't they be blamed for what they cannot help, but their inability to control themselves proves their passionate and virile manliness; it is only their inability to control sinful women that threatens to unman them. Having persuaded themselves of this, they are both more ready to suspect, and more willing to excuse, each other. It is to be expected, for example, that the Prince will swerve from his announced plan, and end up wooing Hero for himself. But the fault is more Hero's than his, according to Claudio, "for beauty is a witch / Against whose charms faith melteth into blood" (2.1.161–62). And though Hero's subsequent betrayal is a heinous crime against the whole Men's Club, Claudio and the Prince find themselves guilty only of a pardonable error in judgment, a position they coolly maintain in the face of Hero's announced death.

The members of the Men's Club are securely joined together by the handcuffs of fashion. "Come," says Dogberry, "let them be opinioned" (4.2.61), and he conspires with his colleagues and Borachio to bring forth their opinionator, the deformed thief, Fashion, who "goes up and down like a gentleman" (3.3.117–18):

BORACHIO: Seest thou not . . . what a deformed thief this fashion is? how giddily 'a turns about all the hot-bloods

> between fourteen and five-and-thirty? sometimes fash-
> ioning them like Pharaoh's soldiers in the reechy paint-
> ing, sometime like god Bel's priests in the old church
> window, sometime like the shaven Hercules in the
> smirched worm-eaten tapestry, where his codpiece seems
> as massy as his club?
>
> (3.3.121–28)

DOGBERRY: And also the watch heard them talk of one
Deformed. They say he wears a key in his ear, and a
lock hanging by it.

(5.1.294–96)

In his stimulating essay on Dogberry, John Allen spells out the rele-
vance of "Borachio's thumbnail sketch of fashion's way with gallants":
"Freely interpreted, fashion first creates the model soldier, gorgeously
arrayed but over-confident and bent on vengeance as a means of
gaining honor; then it supplies him with the outward attributes of one
who cherishes a sacred trust, although he secretly abuses it; and finally
it ushers in his destined role as a uxorious lover, tricked by appetite
into an unmanly servitude which passes for devotion to his female
captor."

> Fashion, as Borachio sees it, signifies the conception of one's
> self which one presents, or wishes to present, to the public
> eye. . . . Like a "deformed thief" . . . fashion steals from
> men their knowledge of themselves, reducing them to pos-
> turing automatons who nourish the illusion of their individu-
> ality while actually possessing none, because they do not
> even choose the fashions they will wear but, whether they
> will or not, are fashioned to them. . . . The spoils of fashion
> are most frequently the qualities . . . which nurture and
> solidify essential interpersonal bonds.

Allen perhaps overstresses the extent to which the play presents men as the slaves of fashion. A clue to their own complicity in fashioning the fashion that robs them is given in Dogberry's
charge to the watch. He tells them that "the most peaceable way"
to keep order is not to interfere with those who disturb the peace.
Item:

> DOGBERRY: If you meet a thief, you may suspect him, by
> virtue of your office, to be no true man; and for such

kind of men, the less you meddle or make with them,
why, the more is for your honesty.

2. WATCH: If we know him to be a thief, shall we not lay
hands on him?

DOGBERRY: Truly, by your office you may; but I think they
that touch pitch will be defiled. The most peaceable
way for you, if you do take a thief, is to let him show
himself what he is, and steal out of your company.

(3.3.47–56)

The Prince had observed in his first speech that "the fashion of the
world is to avoid cost" (1.2.86), and the constable whose office is "to
present the Prince's own person" (3.3.69) agrees: "indeed the watch
ought to offend no man" (3.3.74–75).

Dogberry's instructions for maintaining respectability are worthy
of Erasmus's Folly. The comic paradox giving them their point is that
by refusing to associate with thieves (i.e., refusing to apprehend them)
the watchman becomes their associate. He confirms his illusion of
honesty and joins the community of thieves in one and the same act.
And he is indeed superior to the known thief in his ability to hide his
thievery from himself, to rob himself of self-knowledge, by redistrib-
uting complicities. Avoiding the cost and preserving the peace of the
self-deception Folly called *philautia,* he becomes, like the thief, "no
true man," and he thrives on the ethical confusions of his situation,
confusions which are beautifully expressed in the watch's language:

DOGBERRY: Are you good men and true?

VERGES: Yea, or else it were pity but they should suffer
salvation, body and soul.

DOGBERRY: Nay, that were a punishment too good for
them if they should have any allegiance in them, being
chosen for the Prince's watch.

(3.3.1–6)

It is by meaning and trying to be good men that they both enable
thievery and legitimize their complicity. This does not make them less
good and true; it only suggests that "being good" as Shakespeare
presents it is a more difficult, a more complex and maculate, process
than the purer whole-cloth conception of goodness—and of their own
goodness—entertained by the characters. It seems unavoidable, then,
that Shakespeare's "good" characters should merit salvation and dam-

nation simultaneously. To suffer salvation, to be condemned to redemption, is to suffer the self-deception of *philautia*. Yet this very
illusion of self-esteem is inseparable in most human beings from their
good intentions no less than from the more questionable consequences
of their actions. That the watch should be punished for their allegiance
to the Prince extends this reasoning to the principal characters. The use
of the term *Prince* itself implies this. Since Leonato is listed in the
dramatis personae as the *Governor* of Messina, and Pedro as the *Prince* of
Arragon, "Prince" in this scene comprehends both of these ethically
"vagrom" figures, one the leading elder of the group and the other its
self-confessed love-god. Thus the watch "presents" in its collective
person the principles that underlie and unify the play's two wars—that
is, between generations and between genders. And this extension from
subplot to main plot is manifested in other ways.

According to Dogberry, the ideal watchman is "desartless," liter-
ate, and "senseless," one who can "comprehend all vagrom men" but
can talk himself into releasing them on the grounds that "they are not
the men you took them for" (3.3.8–45). This standard makes "desartless"
an accurate term, fusing "unworthy" with "disingenuous," and it
makes "senseless" mean "self-blinding." Combined with the require-
ment of literacy, the formula produces an exact description of the
members of the Men's Club of Messina. They create and empower the
deformed thief that robs them of the qualities which, in Allen's words,
"nurture and solidify essential interpersonal bonds." Self-robbing thieves
who preserve self-esteem by appropriating Fashion's image, they enable the deformed thief to present their person and go "up and down
like a gentleman," an *arbiter elegantiae*. "Fashion" is roughly synony-
mous with Erasmian folly and *philautia*. It is in part the ability to avoid
cost to oneself by inflicting and blaming it on others. But it is more
than that, as Borachio's words reveal.

Passing from Pharaoh's soldiers through the priests of Bel to the
shaven Hercules, his speech charts a move from war through specious
veneration of an idol to virility unmanned by love. The connection of
Bel to the themes of the play is less apparent, but Shakespeare may
have chosen *Bel* because as the root of both *bellum* and *bella* it provides
an etymological transition while referring to an instance of false devotion directed presumptively toward concern for the idol but actually
toward oneself. The devotion of Cupid's proud subjects is not unlike
that of the priests of Bel. The point of the sequence is borne out by the
general sense that in Messina war and love are interchangeable, because

war is the paradigm of love. Love *of* contention gives way to love *as* contention, and the honeyed rhetoric in which Claudio describes his transformation does not conceal the interchangeability suggested both by his syntax and by his subsequent behavior: now that "war-thoughts / Have left their places vacant, in their rooms / Come thronging soft and delicate desires" (1.1.269–71). The fashion that turns the hot-bloods about reflects their apprehensive reliance on power, their secret worship of self-gratification, and their excessive attachment to *machismo*. But as attempts to avoid cost, these styles of behavior only bring it on; Borachio's examples are all losers, defeated by the true God and woman. And since men were deceivers and self-deceivers ever—since "the fraud of men was ever so"—today's hotblood adopts styles as fusty and worn as the art that communicates them. The Men's Club of Messina can trace its pedigree back to the days of Egypt, Babylon, and Hercules; it adopts and rehabilitates those outworn fashions because it shares the premises of power, cost-avoidance, and fear of love and women that have integrated the male community since summer first was leavy. If the gallants of Messina are doomed to repeat history, it may be because they enjoy their pain. Their chosen fashions betray their misprision of power, their allegiance to the fine art of self-defeat and its long history. Perhaps they avoid cost at one level only to encounter it at another. Like Leonato they come to meet their trouble and embrace their charge too willingly (1.1.85–93). Their club insignia may be the badge of which the messenger spoke: "joy would not show itself modest enough without a badge of bitterness" (1.1.19–21).

If I may digress for a moment to cite a northern analogy, the same bylaws are in effect in the Gloucester chapter of the Gentleman's Club of Old Britain. Gloucester, an old hand at cost-avoidance, tells Kent that Edmund's mother was fair, "there was good sport at his making, and the whoreson must be acknowledged" (1.1.19–23). If that sport smells of any fault, it belongs to the mother for her intemperance and carelessness, and to her son for his saucy disobedience in not remaining nothing. The father's language identifies the mother as a whore, and Edmund not as *his* bastard but as *her* son, and it suggests that mother and son conspired against father in producing the knave before he was sent for. It is thus to father's credit that he overlooks the inconvenience they have caused him, and assumes the consequences of their fault as his own burden: "His breeding, Sir, hath been at my charge" (1.1.8). This piece of bravery is partly a brag, alluding to his notorious accomplishments in lusty stealth, and partly a disclaimer of full responsibility. He seems eager to impress on Kent his paired accomplishments, in good sport and in sportsmanlike conduct. And this, incidentally, may throw some light on the convenient presence in Messina of Don John the Bastard. "Never came trouble to my house in the likeness of your grace" (1.1.88–89), Leonato tells the Prince, and this is because trouble comes in the likeness of Don John, who seems eager to claim even more culpability than he deserves. The Prince drags him around on a leash, like a pet Caliban, so that Don John may receive blame for the trouble which, although it arises from the very foundation of Messina's "dissembly," is orchestrated by Don Pedro's practices. Both brothers, in fact, are practitioners, and the chief difference between them is that the Prince is much better at it.

Don John is a comic villain who can hardly twirl his moustache without scratching his eye. The ease with which this practice (put into play by Borachio and Conrade) succeeds, therefore, tells us more about the susceptibility of Messina than about the Bastard's motiveless malignancy. For the villain to succeed, everyone has to collaborate in helping him on with his bumbling villainies. But this is not something it would be useful for him to find out, for he struts his autonomy and—like Edmund in *King Lear*—takes a certain swashbuckling pride in virile and honorable professions of plain-speaking wickedness, though the pleasure of feeling himself to be a *man,* more sinning than sinned against, is occasionally justified by an appeal to his status as a pariah, more sinned against than sinning. It is sometimes hard to distinguish his own wing of the Men's Club from his brother's. Conrade matches Claudio and Borachio Benedick in the collegiate locker room of wit-crackers, while the latter two show better stuff before the play ends. The play's two scapegoats are a bastard named Trouble and a woman named Hero, and his bastardy tells us where the blame lies: like Edmund, no doubt, he is a testimony both to his father's prowess and to his mother's sin—a by-product of the frailty named Woman.

If this is how men choose to distribute praise and blame, we can understand why they expect women to fail to live up to their responsibilities. If men are deceivers ever, their first deception will be to trick women into loving them. And since women have to be won by the practices of men who flaunt their God-given powers of deception and inconstancy as the jewels of manhood, there is no reason to expect the ladies to honor their commitments. On the other hand, there is no reason not to demand it of them and chastise them when (as is likely) they betray their menfolk into shame. For women are, after all, in a double bond: they are to be wives as well as lovers. That is, they are not only prizes of war, but also commodities in the marriage market. Daughters are ducats. Marriage is a woman's vocation; it is her formal induction into the Men's Club; it is therefore her salvation; to be condemned into everlasting redemption is the fate she was born for. Man, however, was not born for wedlock. It is an accidental inconvenience of the system that after a man has amused himself in hunting his lawful prey, and succeeded in trapping her, he is then expected to deny his nature and spend his life by her side.

Men have, then, a bad conscience about their use and abuse of women in both love and marriage. They know that they do not deserve the loyalty and respect they command women to give them; *they* suspect their place, and they also suspect that *women* do. But this raises a question: If they are apprehensive about their own ability to be good husbands, is it *because* they choose to believe themselves born deceivers, or does it work the other way round? That is, could it be *because* marriage strikes them as a difficult, confining, and dull sink-a-pace that they choose to accept their fate as deceivers who are by nature unfit for it? Like the swan-brides in Spenser's *Prothalamion,* they resist the sink-a-pace because in various ways domesticity presages helplessness and death. For one thing, it means committing their reputation to wives in whom the power of cuckoldry is legally invested. For another, it spells the death of their most precious experience: their companionship with other men. The solidarity of the locker room; the shared vicissitudes of love and war; the easy trust and distrust engendered in friends who are second selves to each other; their common allegiance to self-deception—those are doomed to dissolve after the wedding. Wooing bonds men together in a competitive or cooperative association that marriage threatens; therefore when marriage beckons, men no less than women have to be forcibly separated from the arms of their loved ones. Thus Claudio clings to the Prince before his wedding, begging to escort him to Arragon as soon as the marriage is consummated. At the end of the play, Benedick dallies among his fellow bachelors, and finally, as the turncoats fall away, the Prince sadly stands alone, like the Farmer in the Dell's proverbial cheese.

Male solidarity is never more in evidence than at its twilight. Everyone in the last scene does a Scotch jig to avoid the imminent dispersal through marriage. Benedick and Beatrice resume their earlier roles and seem for a moment ready to shy away from conjugation.

The college of wit-crackers shoot off their last salvo of bad marriage jokes, and reaffirm their commitment to inconstancy. After the events of the fourth act, during which everyone was divided against everyone else, all have succeeded in escaping from that dream of unhappiness-come-true, and now, deceivers ever, they wake themselves with laughing (2.1.308–9) and take their hearing prisoner with the lock of fashion. One after the other, the men rejoin the ranks and redirect their suspicions away from themselves toward the fugitive Don John. At last the Men's Club is back together; but only for a moment. The Club is about to be dismembered. The work—that is, the play—of Leonato, Claudio, and Benedick is over, even the Prince is urged to marry, and all will soon scatter to their newly full or empty households. *Much Ado about Nothing* is an *endless moniment* for short time, and what it celebrates, as the machinery of the sink-a-pace turns over, is the ending of happiness.

This ending begins "aspiciously" enough when Claudio addresses his second wedding as one of the reckonings to be settled, a debt he owes and is owed, or a score he must repay. The first reckoning is with Benedick, who has just genially insulted him:

> CLAUDIO: For this I owe you. Here comes other reck'nings.
>   Which is the lady I must seize upon?
> ANTONIO: This same is she, and I do give you her.
> CLAUDIO: Why, then, she's mine. Sweet, let me see your
>   face.
> LEONATO: No, that you shall not till you take her hand.
>   Before this friar and swear to marry her.
> CLAUDIO: Give me your hand before this holy friar.
>   I am your husband if you like of me.
> HERO: And when I lived I was your other wife;
>   And when you loved you were my other husband.
> CLAUDIO: Another Hero!
> HERO: Nothing certainer.
>   One Hero died defiled; but I do live,
>   And surely as I live, I am a maid.
>
>   (5.4.52–64)

The language emphasizes the forms of *apprehension*. Claudio's is aggressive ("the lady I must seize upon"), Leonato's defensive. Having prayed at her "tomb," the wolves continue to prey (5.3.25). But this time Hero is more than a match for Claudio. The parallels between lines 60 and 61 bring out the biting contrast produced by the difference between "when I *lived*" and "when you *loved*": his "love" is no more real than her "death," and we do not forget that the first marriage failed to take place. Nothing is "certainer" to Hero than that, although she was defiled by slander, her virtue has triumphed over all efforts—and especially over Claudio's—to kill it. Her emphatic assertion of virginity pronounces Claudio guilty. She has the advantage and knows how to call in "other reck'nings." To borrow Portia's words, she capitalizes on "my vantage to exclaim on you" (*Merchant of Venice,* 3.2.174).

Hero makes it clear that the new Hero is simply the old with a vengeance, and though Claudio tries to shuffle off the implication with "*another* Hero," the Prince accepts it: "The former Hero! Hero that is dead!" (5.4.65). Her words reflect mordantly on the friar's self-delighting penchant for staging spiritual scenarios. They remind us that this community harbors no twice-born souls. The friar's practice is a travesty on religious psychology, conversion, and ethical self-transformation. It conspicuously excludes what it parodies, and substitutes a mere plot mechanism equal in ethical quality or causality to the bed trick. His terms of death and rebirth, being metaphorical and counterfactual, work by contraries to affirm that Hero and Claudio remain the same. No one is new-created by verbal or theatrical magic. The dialogue quoted above glances toward the conventional reconciliation. But the parties to it would have to be reborn in a new heaven and earth, a new Messina, before they could enter into a relationship free of the assumptions of their community. Their words, and the friar's game, evoke this possibility only to dispel it. They do not cut through the bond; they only nick it, and the play happily concludes, for *Much Ado* is a Shakespearean comedy—that is, an experience which ends in the nick of time.

Creating a Rational Rinaldo: A Study in the Mixture of the Genres of Comedy and Romance in *Much Ado about Nothing*

John Traugott

A ROMANTICAL-COMICAL FANTASY

Rinaldo, Charlemagne's paladin, shipwrecked on a wild strand of Scotland, though still astride his famous steed Bayard and spoiling for a mission of service to a distressed lady, rides into Messina where the lady Hero having been brutally slandered by her romantic cavalier Claudio (some think him callow) lies dead to the world. He whispers into Claudio's ear, "You are a villain. I jest not. I will make it good how you dare, and when you dare, and her death shall fall heavy on you. Let me hear from you." Claudio thinking he is talking to Benedick the well-known joker returns a quiver of his duller barbs such as "calf's head," "capon," and "woodcock" that express camaraderie in the military ranks. How should he know that Rinaldo has changed himself (for in romance metamorphoses are often possible) into a simulacrum of the rational wit-cracker Benedick who is known to live to mock the posturings of romance? The traduced lady is not dead but only sequestered until something—who knows what?—happens to relieve her of the terrible odium of Claudio's accusation, delivered in a preposterous pet, that he has seen her welcome a man into her window of a murky night. The something that has to happen will be Rinaldo. His metamorphosis into a simulacrum of Benedick has been conjured

From *Genre* 15, nos. 2 & 3 (Spring/Summer 1982). © 1982 by the University of Oklahoma.

up by some clever words of the local virgin wit, Beatrice, whom some think too clever by half. Rinaldo-Benedick knows that Hero is not dead but Claudio does not. He thinks he has killed her with words, but not only is he in a jesting mood with this supposed Benedick, he is as well frolicsome about the poor lady's father and uncle who have finally ventured to defend her honor. "We are like," he jokes, "to have had our two noses [his and Don Pedro's] snapped off with two old men without teeth." What a surprise when "Benedick" turns in contempt from his jests and refers to his sword. Something very odd: the joker has turned as deadly as a knight errant and the romantic cavalier has turned (silly) joker.

From Fantasy to Plot

I will argue that this fantasy is a sketch of Shakespeare's mind working up out of his source in Ariosto the plot of a romantic comedy called *Much Ado about Nothing*. It depends upon the redeployment of the story of Rinaldo's service to Ginevra in the fourth and fifth books of the *Orlando Furioso* and its dramatization comes to a peripety in the "Kill Claudio!" charade Beatrice puts on for Benedick in act 4, scene 1. This scene is therefore the conceptual hinge of the entire action. Here the genre of romance collapses into the genre of comedy, not to forget its dreams of service and love and derring-do (nor to escape its vocation for violence), but to lend those dreams to the fantasies of triumph of a comic action. How we get to this scene and what happens in it is a study that yields a good understanding of the agency of romance in comedy and the effects Shakespeare was seeking by the "contamination" of the genres, matters crucial to the production and acting of this difficult comedy.

Ariosto's story falls together with another from Bandello's *Novelle,* the twentieth, similar but with crucial differences in event and feeling. In Bandello there is no Rinaldo; the lady is traduced but she gets no service. Rather, an access of sentimental remorse in the villain permits her resuscitation. In any case Rinaldo with his aura of romantic magic about him would cut a bizarre figure in the domestic purlieus of Bandello's Messina. Although the borrowings from the sources were long ago traced out by scholarship, the remaking of Rinaldo's knight errantry has not been remarked, so bizarre is this metamorphosis of the romance here into the wit-cracker, and yet I take that strange turn to be the crux of the play. Following through Shakespeare's reworking of these sources, "making strange" and "laying bare" (to borrow Shklovski's useful formula) the conventions of romance, we have a singular opportunity to reflect on the moral puzzles and mystifications hidden in the very dreams of romance—what we may call its grace with disgrace—that Shakespeare seems obsessively to unveil. And it is this very double mindedness of romance that invites its "contamination" by comedy. Its grace will render comedy a new sort of triumph over a scurvy world, its violences and absurdities will have to endure laughter. Swift speaks of platonics with their eyes fixed on the stars seduced by their lower parts to a ditch (*Mechanical Operation of the Spirit*). Shakespeare as dearly loves a low-down sexual pun as Swift but his subject is not the lower parts. "The revolt of a codpiece," yes, the savvy rascal Lucio speaking for once for the play, but for Shakespeare the revolt is only human, not bestial, and likely to come upon us all. Rather it is the violence hidden in romantic yearnings for absolute love that fascinates Shakespeare—but fascinates him no more than the gentle and gracious ideal of service that goes with the yearnings. And the interplay of the roles prescribed by romance with those of comedy is one more working out of his recurrent metaphysic that we are all perforce players in one play or another; in the case of *Much Ado* players in two plays at once. *Much Ado* is almost made up of set skits of the fixed roles of romance and of comedy—the Beatrice-Benedick slanging match, braggart warrior and shrew, of the opening; the masked ball of romantic and comic mistaken identities; the put-on of the eavesdropping scenes; the window trick enraging the jealous lover; the "rotten orange" show staged by the betrayed lover; the "kill Claudio!" scene of the knight's service to the distressed lady; the contrition at graveside of the desolate lover; and the unveiling masque of romantic magic at the end. If the world is to be represented as comedy, then the greatest exhilaration and joy must live in a player's mastery of his (her) role, gaining his freedom, directing the action to make things come out right. As it is Beatrice who gives Benedick his lessons in the opportunities of his role, it is she who is in custody of our comic pleasure and whom we must attend. She is the surrogate playwright.

"KILL CLAUDIO!"—JOKE OR SENTIMENT

"Kill Claudio!" Beatrice to Benedick. Two wit-crackers who have nothing to do but parody the romance code summed up in Beatrice's fleering insult to Benedick early on, "a soldier to a lady," the code with which their author has afflicted everyone else in the play. They seem now suddenly to have themselves taken on the histrionics of that code. Romance has come to a pretty pass—an innocent lady traduced by this callow cavalier of a Claudio returned from the wars billed as better than the promise of his age, the figure of a lamb doing the feats of a lion. Romance little knows what it promises or what beast may lurk in the figure of a lamb. One moment he is worshipping at Hero's shrine from afar, a timorous hangdog of an absolute lover, struck dumb by the apparition of the lady and requiring an intermediary to do his business, the next skulking and brooding, desolated and despairing, in his imagined rejection. And then infected by the breath of a nasty tale, playing the voyeur to collect specious evidence of his betrayal, he is suddenly indulging a rage of sexual sadism that anywhere but in a romance would mark him out as demented. This man has all the marks of the romance code on him. This lady needs a champion. But "Kill Claudio!"? That imperious command might come from a lady in a high romance, but from Beatrice, the only one in the cast who "can see a church by daylight"? She employs a knight errant to do her jousting and slashing for her? Bizarre. Is it intended to collapse all this claptrap of romance by parody—just another of Beatrice's charades, this time burlesquing the code obliging a traduced virgin to die and equally obliging a stray knight wandering upon the scene to throw down the gauntlet to vindicate her honor so that she need not die after all! Or is it to be played as a thrill of sincerity, signalling the wit-crackers' capitulation to the code, their giving up of game as the rule of life? Is this Beatrice, caught out in the earlier eavesdropping scene, her virgin's heart, hitherto stifled beneath the armor of maidenly pride, exposed, now to be reduced to the banality of woman, astringent humors purged away? "Methinks," says Margaret cattily, "you look with your eyes as other women do." Margaret makes remarks. She is something of a counter-wit to Beatrice. She knows a thing or two about metaphors of swords and bucklers and pikes screwed in with a vice. Beatrice has her supply of such metaphors but she does not look as other women do. They look. She sees.

Joke or sentiment? Good actresses play it for laughs and other good ones play it for sentiment. Is this a time for jokes when romance has taken, as is its wont in Shakespeare, a sudden turn from the nobleness of life to degrading violence, including a squalid cynicism about female sexuality? No reason to think this is not a serious matter. Claudio is, as we shall see, an apprentice Othello. In another genre he would kill someone. On the other hand, for Beatrice and Benedick to give up game for the single-heartedness that is called "sincerity" would be to abandon their intellectual mastery of the romance-mad world they are obliged to live in and their talent for creating their lives by the arts of language. Write off Beatrice as a shrew who has amusingly been brought down to the banality of woman and the drama of the code of game against the code of romances collapses, and with it the playwright's astonishing metamorphosis of Rinaldo into Benedick. Something more than tumbling Jack with Jill is needed for the ending. We need a rational Rinaldo and a worldly Ginevra. Improbable brave new world. But comedy requires improbability—as we shall see. How to play this improbable contamination of the genres upon a stage?

GRACE AND DISGRACE IN THE CODE

Let us return to the sources. We rejoin Rinaldo ahorseback in a dark wood. *Désoeuvré*, he requires chivalric employment. The code calls into being its own world. Old religious men appear to tell him the story of Ginevra, the maiden who must die at St. Andrews should a champion not appear to defend her honor. Has she played her intended, Ariodant, false and become whore to his erstwhile friend Polynesso, as charged? The question of Ginevra's chastity, so terrible to her, is almost indifferent to Rinaldo. No Scottish moralist, he supposes that a woman will have desires as well as a man. Would that they could get away with the expression of them.

Thus Ariosto furnishes two versions of the romance code for Shakespeare's story of the distressed lady. One, Rinaldo's, not overcurious about her status as *virgo intacta* but calculated to render her service in her most need; the other, St. Andrews's, obsessed by the glory of the gossamer redoubt of virginity. The glory, according to the code, has death in it. The lady, her accuser, her champion—one or more of them must die upon the mere imputation of unchastity. Beatrice and Benedick appropriate Rinaldo's version of service; Claudio, St. Andrews's of violent retribution. This lady is indeed in distress; service is the thing. That determined, Rinaldo straightaway comes upon miscreants about to do in Dalinda, the lady's maid servant. She tells her story of the window trick by which at Polynesso's behest she impersonated her mistress while receiving him at her window, a show intended to desolate Ariodant the lover. For her pains in helping him to her mistress, Polynesso has sent his minions to shut her mouth forever.

Dalinda then becomes Margaret, Ginevra Hero, but Polynesso has disappeared. His accomplished villainy is given over to Don John, the cardboard nasty, his sexual involvement with the lady's maid to Borachio, Don John's agent. Unlike Ariodant, who is the noble victim of his rival Polynesso, Claudio has no rival except the phantom created by the window trick, and that is just Don John's way of indulging his mindless malice. but Claudio, never having had a rival, accepts the illusion of one so easily that he seems to have been awaiting betrayal as the fate of absolute lovers like himself. If he will believe Don John he will believe anything that suits his role as lover by the romance code. Polynesso, according to Ariosto is a "hound of hell," someone to reckon with, but Don John comes onstage announcing himself as a comic heavy, a canker in a hedge, a plain-dealing villain, to be trusted only when muzzled, dragging a ball and chain, and behind bars. No deception there, no hypocrisy. But good enough for Claudio, and even for his go-between, Don Pedro, who here is just acting out his role according to the code. Don John's window trick is reported, not represented, because the whole mix-up needs to be as little plausible as possible, a confection of the mind.

"Hear me call Margaret Hero and hear Margaret term me Claudio," says Borachio of his plan. Editors have sometimes written bemused glosses to this line. Did Shakespeare slip here? Is "Borachio" meant for "Claudio"? But of course an emendation makes hash of the dramatic truth here. For Borachio is clearly intending to get up a lover's game with Margaret. Lovers love to tease and pleasure one another by playing mock roles and she will easily be led on to play her mistress to Borachio's Claudio. Her "Claudio" will fall on Claudio's ears as a deliberate taunting of him as a fatuous lover. He will think himself mocked, just the thing to induce the insane fear of betrayal likely to inhabit romantic love.

The Shakespearean rewriting of the story deliberately weakens motivations, making the deception so crude that Claudio's credulousness betrays his affliction. Don John is in little need of the talent for villainy he doesn't have. All this heightens the audience's awareness of the violence and cruelty hidden in the wild imaginings of romance.

The borrowings from Bandello have a similar effect by transferring romance from its native never-never land of wild strands, dark forests, and remote redoubts where maidens suffer strange practices to the mentality of otherwise household characters. The soldiers returned from the wars to woo the marriageable daughters of the governor's household, their families eager to dispose of them, the sentimental hullabaloo of the false accusation, the sequestration of the lady with the report of her death by the shamed family, the tearful contrition of the disabused lover before the "tomb," and her "miraculous" revival for the marriage as originally planned—all this domesticity borrowed from Bandello also makes romance less a thing of wonder than a personality disorder of everyday life in our culture.

From the manipulation of sources then come the various images of the romance code. That the code has its irresistible graces is a belief as banal in our day as in Shakespeare's. Service to the lady (whether she be helpless or imperious, a Hero or a Beatrice), courage to create oneself as the embodiment of honor, derring-do and adventure in the lists of Good—these are principles that defeat the fear of death—if one doesn't think too much of the event. Even the reading of *Amadis de Gaule,* says Sidney (*Apologie for Poetrie*) has moved men's hearts to the exercise of courtesy, liberality, and especially courage.

If, however, one can see a church by daylight, other images appear. Some of violence, some of absurdity, or of both together. Now the love of love is the love of death, service to the lady an opportunity for mayhem, and the lady, bearing such a heavy responsibility to ennoble the lover, likely to betray him whatever she does. Only want of ingenuity tempers cruelty. And these deadly qualities are equalled by the comic absurdities of the postures enforced by the code.

Shakespeare never tires of these jests. Feste sardonically glossing his own song about love sung to assuage Orsino's oceanic love of love, says *sotto voce* that such men ought to be put to sea that their business may be everywhere, their intent nowhere, making a good voyage of nothing. Puck thinks he will be an actor in the sport proving that everyone loves an ass when the dream of love with its apparatus of potions, love to the death, and terror of betrayal gets into the brain. Rosalind tells the truth that disdainful ladies are not necessarily for all markets: "sell when you can." Desdemona is sure she would not do the deed of darkness "for all the world." Emilia thinks she might do it "for all the world": "It is a great price for a small vice." "Not by this heavenly light," says Desdemona. "No, you can do't as well i'th' dark," says Emilia.

The grace, the cruelty, and the jest. All this is Shakespeare's romance. Romance has a vocation for cruelty but comedy can cure it. *Othello* and *Much Ado* are two versions of the same code. What technique of murder would Claudio have employed had Don John told him of ladders and windows after his marriage to Hero? His ocular proof is about in the same class with Othello's handkerchief. No need to see a church by daylight when one had an idea in the head to give inward vision. Perhaps Iago is overrated: when an Othello has an idea of his wife as "monumental alabaster" it is not so remarkable that a joker like Iago can turn him into a fool. As Emilia says, he is "ignorant as dirt," he is a "gull," he is a "dolt," he is a "dull Moor." And he is by his own just estimate, a "fool, fool, fool!" There is something in T. S. Eliot's contention that in his "noble" maunderings after the catastrophe, Othello is just talking to cheer himself up. Othello and Claudio are equally dangerous and for the same reason, that they are fools to the code of romance. They are equally bad jokes. Only the genre makes the difference. Beatrice and Benedick are jokers who reduce the code of romance to their code of game; Iago is a joker who reduced the code to death. The code has game hidden in it; it has death hidden in it. Only the genre makes the difference.

Othello and *Much Ado,* despite the wild imaginings of the "soldier to a lady" in each, are fundamentally domestic plays. The violence of the romantic claim of the ideal is driven into the minds of people of this world who live not too far from the home place of the audience. There, while the household is abustle about the business of getting the young woman married off, while titters about sexuality witness the banality of the proceedings, the demon that is the idea is preparing his scenes of hysteria. In *Much Ado* the borrowings from Bandello make the framework of the domesticized romance. But the "Kill Claudio!" scene comes from a purer strain of romance and has no domestic coloring. Ariosto has nothing to do with households or with getting young women properly married off. Rinaldo's championing of the lady who must die is gratuitous generosity, service pure and simple. That sort of thing happens in the never-never land of romance; it has no counterpart in Bandello. What is so startling then in the "Kill Claudio!" scene—and essential to the working out of the comic fantasy of triumph—is the displacement of this purer element from the strange landscape of romance to the worldly preserve Beatrice and Benedick have made for themselves in Messina by their game parodying and mocking the domestic remains of romance. Suddenly our expectations are derailed and they have stolen away the convention of service to the distressed lady, together with its man on horseback, its idealism, its grace, and incongruously incorporated it in the comic charades they concoct between themselves. The wit plot has absorbed the romance plot. Beatrice dubs Benedick a rational Rinaldo. Only one problem: in the process of saving romance for reason, she has set going an action, the challenge, the duel that must follow, which will be more violence, more disgrace of romance. But the genre of comedy can cure that.

CLAUDIO'S ROMANTIC SINCERITY

Beatrice's command of service need not then be taken as newfound "sincerity." If that word means anything in the context of a comic action that has everyone playing roles and not spilling souls, it can only mean that the role is inflexible, a pose that must entrain willy-nilly predictable and logical consequences. The mastery of a role on the contrary will never be "sincere" since it requires the conscious use of role to make the play come out right. To be sincere is to be one thing; Beatrice is far from that. In appropriating the code of romance to her own uses there is something new but it is still a game, only a game turned to isolating Claudio and his weird shenanigans beyond the pale so that people can get on with living. It is a stagey piece of rhetorical play got up for this moment of the drama when romance has found its level, murderous absurdity, and something has to be done to save the cast from sinking into stupidity. She does her rhetorical tricks with Benedick until he is willing to play the Rinaldo despite his good eyesight, and she has at the same time worded herself into the role of a worldly Ginevra. Appropriating romance to her game-playing, she takes her place with other Shakespearean wonder women who know how to save a plot gone into impasse by becoming surrogate play-wrights, putting on the actors to make things come out right, as their author made them know it must do.

How did the play come to this impasse? Beatrice and Benedick have very little to do with it. They are just stopping time with their games; it is Claudio who is moving the plot—through every cliché in the book of romance. He is stupefied by a sublimity of a Hero on the far side of the stage: "Can the world buy such a jewel?" That is the reach of his conversation. He needs an intermediary. Benedick isn't much help. He sees on the other side of the stage "Leonato's short daughter." But he can turn words. "Yes, and a case to put it in too." Yes, you can buy a female ("jewel") and with the purchase a genital ("case") to put your genital ("it") in. Such rude reduction is not much help to a high flyer like Claudio but some help to the play which continually returns sublimities to their original earthiness.

As an intermediary is requisite in romance (Orsino, Troilus, Orlando, Armado, and Othello, among others, require one), Don Pedro takes on the job. But Don John has only to do his little villain's jig at the masquerade ball, saying to Claudio that Don Pedro woos Hero for himself and Claudio is instantly despairing: "Farewell, Hero, farewell." And when Benedick twits him with the same suggestion, he goes further into the sulks because he has to play the desolate lover of romance.

Claudio does not really know what he is brooding on but the play does. Unbeknownst to himself, he is getting himself up for his grand scene of mad lover, *Claudio furioso,* violent and dangerous, who fancies himself betrayed by a lady with whom he has exchanged no more than a word. Next he is spying, playing the voyeur at Hero's window at night, when, says Don John (who has warned the audience not to trust him), she has a lover climbing up a ladder. Again Claudio looks but doesn't see, but what use are eyes to see with when one has inner vision? "Talk with a man out at a window!" says Beatrice with anger and disgust at his preposterous presumptions. Claudio must be played with a certain mooncalf charm—otherwise marrying him off to a resuscitated Hero at the end is intolerable—but what a dangerous fool he is when his romance-in-the-head authorizes him to run amok.

He is ready for his grand scene. In this scenario Hero has known the heat of a luxurious bed a thousand times. That according to Borachio's "confession." A thousand times? Three years of climbing nocturnal ladders, reckoning in occasional indispositions. And that's not all. Sodomy too. This seeming Diana is a Venus and more intemperate than pet animals kept for savage sensuality. And that's not all. She is a common stale. Common? Were there other men at other ladders to other windows? If this sort of rant occurred in tragedy the audience would guffaw—all this ladder climbing, romping with animals, heating luxuriously night in and night out. (*Othello* edges on the same absurdity. Again, Othello seems to have apprenticed as Claudio. He uses the same figure: Desdemona has done it a thousand times. This Othello is, as Emilia says, a dolt, but we do not guffaw because the noble Othello of the beginning is all the more present by his absence at the end.) But here laughter is preempted by the wit game, and moreover this absurdity of Claudio's, as it is meant to kill and in a caddish way, is disgusting. Someone must take charge of these romance-mad fools. How else then to challenge Claudio? Surely the office of a hero of romance. Charlemagne's paladin Rinaldo who has been waiting in the wings is called in, given the guise of Benedick, and wit and romance flourish in one person.

To revenge his "betrayal" Claudio has prepared for the wedding the ritual sacrifice of Hero. He knows the code. The procession files into the church, the friar starts up the ceremony. "You come hither to marry this lady?" "No!" The purport of the question is explained to him. No answer. The friar turns to Hero, as though he hasn't heard Claudio's silence. She is a proper girl; she knows the right answer. Any inward impediments? asks the friar. Leonato answers hastily to head off more of Claudio's mysterious shenanigans. "I dare make his answer—none." It is all happening just as though Claudio had written the dialogue. Now he is ready for the peripety. He apostrophizes the world, or perhaps the universe: "O what men dare do! What men daily do! What men may do! Not knowing what they do!"

Benedick gets into the act, desperately trying to turn Claudio's outbursts into a comic routine. "Interjections? Why then some be of laughing, as 'ah he he!' " Is this a tragical romance or a romantical comedy? Like Polonius, Shakespeare is known for mixing genres: same action, different codes.

Now Claudio goes into his grand tirade: "There Leonato, take her back again / Give not this rotten orange to your friend." The stage business requires violence. For Claudio to throw Hero at her father would point the drama of his easy "murder" against Benedick's desperate laughter. This is the moment of Claudio's recital of Hero's wild sexual licence.

Who would believe it? Everyone—except the custodians of the other code, Beatrice and Benedick. Don Pedro, otherwise good humored, easily participates in the madness, as does even poor Hero's father Leonato who comforts his daughter by telling her to die again after she has revived from the swoon everyone thought must be her death.

Whether or not de Rougemont is right that courtly love has a congenital connection with the heresy of the Cathars, bespeaking its dreaming on the ineffable woman, its seeking forever the portal of death to otherworldliness (*Passion and Society*), there is no doubt that the "soldier to a lady" (played by Claudio, grotesquely parodied by Benedict) has a vocation for whatever will prevent the ordinary, workaday relation between the sexes. It is only a "little peg," says Rabelais, that connects the sexes. Romance will speak of nothing so simple and vulgar as that. Heroes of antiromance—or sanity—such as Rabelais and Swift, have had to resort to flinging dung to remind the sexes of their ineffability. That is one way to cure us of romance. Another way is the tradition of English wit comedy founded by Beatrice in which the ineffable lady and all the romantic postures are parodied by precious ladies who have good fun parodying themselves. In this comedy the daughters of Beatrice manage to bring off the coup of amalgamating the grace of romance, respecting the pleasures of femininity, with the debunking of its irrational vocation for death and destruction. Beatrice could have cured Romeo: "I will believe, / Shall I believe? that unsubstantial death is amorous? / And that the lean abhorred monster keeps / Thee here in the dark to be his paramour?" The answer to the question is Beatrice's answer to Benedick's question whether she loves him. "No more than reason." Claudio's question about Hero, "Can the world buy such a jewel?" is answered by Millamant: she will not be called names—like "jewel" and "the rest of that nauseous cant." All the same this daughter of Beatrice will have her fanciful demands for service and adoration respected—within reason. It was Beatrice who invented this purloining of the grace of romance for the cause of reason in the congress of the sexes, parodying and ridiculing away its pretension to otherworldliness. It was Beatrice who made possible Congreve's attribution of the "dyingness" of romance to Lady Wishfort, a grotesque crone always wishing for "it" behind a maquillage like "cream cheese."

If we delve into the recesses of the myth of love in romance, says de Rougemont, we see that obstruction to fulfillment is what passion wants, lest it be dissipated in worldliness. A question or two would have cleared up Claudio's purblind visions of his betrayal, but as de Rougemont says of Tristan, "honor supervenes" and Claudio is ready to believe that Hero must die because she doesn't measure up to a jewel that all the world could not buy. All this may seem too much to deliver upon the shoulders of a mooncalf like Claudio, indeed a very attenuated Tristan, until one reflects that the drama the mooncalf is getting up, the pomp and ceremony and especially the high rhetoric, "your Hero, my Hero, everyman's Hero," will justify his violence. The feats of the hero of romance are feats that only a Manichaean world can demand, the seeking of the absolute good, the extirpation of all else. Good is the thrall of evil. No cruel Scottish code, no knight-errantry for Rinaldo. Evil is as well the thrall of good. No jewel, no rotten orange. We are always coming back to square one.

THE CODE OF GAME

But in *Much Ado* we are not, after all, in the crepuscular glooms of the medieval forests of Scotland, nor on the windswept plateau of Les Baux. The code of chivalric love, says C. S. Lewis, is the feudalization of love, but we are in the Elizabethan absolute monarchy, lords beware, in which love is supposed to have its place not in adulterous service to a lady but in marriage, a sacrament and a political instrument parallel to the state. Romance must find a domestic place, a contradiction in terms. Claudio is quite domestic—he wants to make sure of his dowry before he begins to play out the romance—but he wants his absolutes, too, that will obstruct the marriage. Such paradoxes are resolved in comedy in which you have your cake and eat it too. The model lovers' dialogues of Andreas, which are concerned with the practical matter of getting lovers together according to the rules and reflect none of the mystique de Rougemont traces to the Cathars, are already touched by the comic, inadvertent though it may be, as just to turn words in such casuistry is an incipient game. The man says that he must love in order to do good deeds, love being their inspiration. The woman says he must do good deeds in order to have her love, love being their reward. If what she says is true, he says, society will be deprived of good deeds as love makes men good and good men do good deeds. If what he says is true, she says, those who do no good deeds will have love before those who do good deeds, the former having plenty of time at their disposal and the latter being busy (*Art of Courtly Love*).

Once such debate gets going, the end of the line will be the slanging matches of a Beatrice and Benedick. They have only to learn to use it for their own ends. However narcissistic they may seem in pleasuring themselves by linguistic play, they must in fact be heroic just to keep up their game—playing when love has so many perils in Messina.

Game is in itself innocent of moral purpose and these sophisticates Beatrice and Benedick are great innocents. By their parody of the code of romance they have in mind only to keep themselves clear of the whole business—which Beatrice sees as a dance of death. And what do they know of one another? The parody is something they can do together while staying apart. They are, nonetheless, almost unawares changing worlds, contaminating one literary genre with another (to the benefit of both), and redoing romance for the imagination of the life we must live.

Their game is a set of charades unable to become a play, just variations on a theme. It has the pleasure of role-playing, keeping them free of prescribed roles and received ideas. They write the dialogue and play the parts in an intuitive but offhand collaboration. She will be "Lady Disdain," speaking "poniards"; he "Signior Mountanto." "I pray you, is Signior Mountanto returned from the wars or no?" She means "Signior Upthrust," referring to a flamboyant maneuver of fencing, but as she is immediately calling him "a soldier to a lady," she has in mind also that the paladin of romance is likely to turn out to be the braggart warrior (which classically includes a sexual swagger) of the old comedy. Benedick cuts up the air with his foil like Hotspur—"I pray you, how many hath he killed and eaten in these wars?"—asks Beatrice, playing the female echo to Prince Hal. (Chivalry and comedy were a pair running in Shakespeare's head in these two plays of about a year apart.) Benedick has been inventing routines to keep the braggart warrior skit going, challenging Cupid in a match of love archery, taking on the fool as Cupid's stand-in. In all these braggadocio charades there is an edge of violence and morbidity. Killing and eating, blinding (if I die for love pick out my eyes with a ballad-maker's pen), hanging (hang me up at the door of a brothel for the sign of blind Cupid), sporting cruelty (hang me in a bottle like a cat and shoot at me). Beatrice will be a "curst cow" and an ape ward in hell, a corpse in her grave before lying between marriage sheets (better to "lie in the woolen," the burial shroud), the sexual victim ("overmastered") of a vain cavalier who will be no more to her than his eventual corpse ("piece of valiant dust"), a dancer in the dance of death that is wooing (jig), wedding (measure), and repenting (cinque-a-pace) faster and faster into the grave. To be a lover is as good as seeking torture or death. What a pair of jokers! Are they warding off the worst Messina can do with its romance code? Have they not good reason for these black jokes? Humor, says Freud, is a sort of short circuit of feeling, it saves the energy that would be expended if one were to take reality seriously. "The grandeur of [humor] lies in the triumph of narcissism, the victorious assertion of the ego's invulnerability. The ego refuses to be distressed by the provocations of reality, to let itself be compelled to suffer. . . . [Humor] means: 'Look! Here is the world, which seems so dangerous. It is nothing but a game for children—just worth making a jest about!' " This definition has its own truth, no need to bring down the psychoanalytic paraphernalia on these two jokers; they have no psyches, just their sense of role and their wit. They love their own wit first of all and refuse to take seriously the provocations of the romance code with its threats of torture and death. It is just a game for children.

So Benedick plays the braggart warrior and Beatrice plays the shrew of the old comedy. Neither, however, is playing the role straight; both are parodying, playing to their own dialogue; both are comic playwrights. Playing to his partner, Benedick does his routine of a "squarer" (title courtesy of Beatrice), infecting his fellow bully-boys with the "Benedick." "It is certain I am loved of all the ladies, only you excepted," says he on cue. Killer, lady-killer, Signior Upthrust. Even Leonato is enrolled for a moment in the game, playing *bonhomme* with a horn joke on himself to Benedick's greater glory: he is sure Hero is his daughter because Signior Benedick was then a child. A poor joke but his own, showing at least that Benedick's role is a recreation for everyone.

Mimicked by them the code of romance is transmuted into "time-out," game-time, whereas for the rest of the cast it is "forever and a day," the very life-time. Game has its own time and space discontinuous with that of biological life. It goes by rules and towards a goal within the game, even if, as in this case, the goal is only to keep up the play. Game puts a simplified order on some part of "life." It tidies up the systems of behavior—war, business, love, and so on—that seem always to be tending towards chaos. Games are recreation by which one can forget the gravity that infects systems in real time and space. They are never thought to correspond to some inherent order in the universe, they have no commitments, no consequences, no teleologies. The player is never "sincere"; he is only playing. He is not afflicted with a personality prescribed by society, only a part in the game. A player who makes up his own game and can get others to play it can invent any role for himself he chooses. Beatrice plays the shrew, Benedick the braggart warrior, but comically and parodically, and they make up the shrew-braggart warrior game together. They see no end to it. Beatrice would join the unmarried jokers in heaven; Benedick invents terrible cruelties to suffer if he gives up.

That is how they talk, but for all their talk their game—like all games—is not really separable from the life enveloping it. How should it be? They are skating on thin ice, every scene shows it. Their own wit, however enjoyable to themselves and others, is repetitive and offers no way out. Yet they are reasonable and must resist the absurdities and finally the cruelties of the romance code that encloses them. Nor can they yield to the gambits of others to sentimentalize them into

Jack and Jill. Their game is an unstable equilibrium threatened by forces without and within. But that is the way with game and it is worth a short detour to consider philosophically why it is unlikely to continue long without infecting or being infected by the life surrounding.

Almost any code of behavior is a "game" in a skewed but popular sense of that word—"the political game," "the sex game," "the patriot game," and so on. Why is the romance code of Hero and Claudio not a "game" as well as the "wit game" of Beatrice and Benedick? Romance, even if it kills its heroes or translates them to eternal felicity, a wild teleology that seems alien to game, looks like a game in other characteristic ways. It is rule-bound and tries to delimit its own time and space—"Had we but world enough and time, / This coyness, lady were no crime." Such applications of "game" easily become larger and larger, vaguer and vaguer, but they have a kind of sense. Still, absolutely considered, definitions should stay within bounds, and one of the boundaries of game is that it has no teleology either in biological life or in "the order of things." But teleology is hard to shut out. It enters where it is least wanted—a touch of pomposity and it is there: the battle of Waterloo was won on the playing fields of Eton—and such. That pomposity being uttered, no game on the playing fields of Eton could thereafter be a game pure and simple. Not even pomposity is required. Stendhal's court of Parma shows how political games necessarily seek the destruction of life. Swift's Lilliput likewise. And Shakespeare's history plays dance out their mystique of kingship on a high wire between game and divinity.

For as the players live in biological time along with nonplayers and occupy with them the same space filled with the reticulations of human relations—a space full of elbows—they will necessarily break down the disjunctions between time and space inside and outside the game. Life will spill into game, corrupting it, making the rules and goals of the game as unrecreational as possible, and with a vengeance. And game will spill into life, trivializing it. Game, furthermore, has its uses going quite beyond recreation. It provides, for example, "leeway" by which decisions calling for irreversible actions can be postponed long enough to allow the imagination to try out roles and attitudes relating the self and the other. It is protection, a kind of deer park for the self, when commitment in real time and space may cause one to enter on a dangerous hunting ground. It is a way of knowing qualities of mind and heart of other players, possibly a crucial matter if one has to live with them when the game ends. And in other ways too game and life tend to encroach uncomfortably on one another, but those mentioned serve to give a perspective on what Beatrice and Benedick are up to.

The undefined edges of "game" in its philosophical construction define paradoxically the address and talent with which they move through their verbal stunts to keep their own time and space disjunctive to that of the surrounding romance code. Their recreation is their salvation from pompous, deadening, and perhaps killing teleologies. If life must at last dissolve the edges of their game, they want to keep the process under their own control. They grow testy at Claudio's silly, good-fellow jokes in the midst of his outrages to reason, for they are a trivial parody of themselves. They do not mean to give up at the end, for all the matings, their stylish wit game that keeps romance at its proper distance.

But they cannot move the plot. For all the domestic talk about marriages and dowers and proper behavior between the sexes, it is the absolutism of the romance code that causes the action. The "horn jokes" that punctuate the dialogue from first to last—"But when shall we set the salvage bull's horns on the sensible Benedick's head," and so on—though tiresome, tell of the undercurrent of sexual fear running in the code; one knows that one has married the perfect woman because every other woman is an adultress; what a noble trust one has!; woe be to her that betrays it! The plot is assured. Beatrice and Benedick can't keep up their game forever to ward off this murderous absurdity; sooner or later they will be bedded down along with the rest. What terms can be made between the high-flying pretensions and the low-down realities of sexuality? Beatrice is obsessed, as is the play with its horn jokes, by this disjunction. She is forever thinking of (or being made to think of) the ultimate female position in the congress of the sexes—put down, overmastered, lying in woolen, dancing the love dance down into the grave, singing the ballad "light a Love" without a burden (the weight of a husband), dancing the same ballad with her heels (in bed), "stuffed," "pricked" by the thistle "benedictus." The high-flying and the low-down in Messina. Reason enough to keep up the game.

But smart talk forever? The eavesdropping scenes engineered by Don Pedro have already allowed them to drop the shrew-braggart warrior parodies. Benedick has been made to overhear the gossip that Beatrice has written "Beatrice and Benedick" on a sheet of paper and got up a joke about finding Beatrice and Benedick between the sheets. And she has been made to overhear the talk that Benedick deserves as "fortunate a bed as Beatrice couches on." Both having been fitted for bed, each puts on a little theatre, Benedick an apostrophe to demography ("The world must be peopled"), Beatrice a piece of pindaric, ten lines with rhyme ("Contempt farewell and maiden pride adieu! . . . Benedick love on"). They take the way out offered but they do not turn romantic, much less sentimental, and their sense of theatre is unchanged.

But when they next come on stage the romance code has discovered its vocation for violence. Claudio has fulfilled his role; for all he knows Hero is dead, and justly, because he has an idea in his head that seeming Dianas are really Venuses and are likely to betray the absolute love of cavaliers like himself. A new kind of theatre is required. Beatrice, starting up a new game, manages the stunt of bringing romance to the service of reason.

Friar Francis has been bustling about setting on foot a plan to sequester poor Hero. Perhaps she will prove innocent. Perhaps Claudio will repent of his sadism. Perhaps people will forget in time. If none of these she can always be shut up in a nunnery. Such a heap of pious clichés cannot be congenial to Beatrice, who sets up to look at the obvious. As for Hero she cannot say more for herself than that she hopes to be tortured if there was a man at her room.

Who would not weep to hear such stuff? No one, except Beatrice, and her weeping is clearly part of a rhetorical game she decides to play with Benedick to set the world right.

She weeps and Benedick is moved to agree that Hero must be wronged. Her scenario is begun. "Ah, how much might the man deserve of me that would right her!" When before has she taken the posture of the lady who will requite chivalric service? New part, new rhetoric. Benedick has left off his braggart warrior performance and professed love. She will turn the new look of things to account. "It is a man's office but not yours." Strange, says he, that he loves her. As strange, says she, that she might love him. "I confess nothing, nor I deny nothing. I am sorry for my cousin." Sincerity is also good theatre. Benedick returns to a memory of his role as braggart warrior and lady killer, showing off his equipment: "By my sword, Beatrice, thou lov'st me." She uses that: Do not swear by it and eat it. "God forgive me . . . I was about to protest I loved you." Do. I do. "Come, bid me do anything for you." Back to the courts of love. It has as well the ring of proud lovers dancing out their pride before making the inevitable arrangements. But it is not so for her: neither the courts of love nor the prideful dance. She is dancing out a rhetoric, preparing a peripety of complete surprise against which he will be wholly disarmed despite his flourishing sword. "Kill Claudio!"

Imperious airs of the lady of a high romance ordaining that her paladin ride off to snickersnack the bandersnatch. A rhetorical mousetrap for this joker. As he is accustomed to doing a parody of the braggart warrior, for the sport, now if he refuses the order he will not be a parody of the braggart warrior but the braggart warrior himself. But she must be joking. "Ha, not for the wide world." "You kill me to deny it. Farewell . . . I am gone though I am here." Is she serious? She pulls out another stop, a noble rage against Claudios (and Benedicks if they choose the category) and all candy counts playing at undying love. "Princes and counties! . . . Count Comfect." Gallants, curtsies, complements. "Tarry, good Beatrice. By this hand, I love thee." "Use it for my love some other way than by swearing by it." "I will challenge him."

What else if he is not to become in fact a type figure of the old comedy blathering on forever about how the ladies love him? The conceptual plot turns here. Beatrice must be felt to be ordering a scurvy world, invading it to enforce her rational analyses worked out in the time and space reserved to her game with Benedick. But with an original turn. She has not only brought play to redress a world that has no sense in it but has stolen away its best pretensions—to service, to sacrifice, to loyalty—to grace her own play in the service of reason. She has made a rational Rinaldo of Benedick, a worldly Ginevra of herself.

Claudio has the luck to find himself in a comedy, not a romance. Otherwise it would come to swords. Thanks to the will of Beatrice and Benedick to play their game parodying the postures of romance and then to steal away its idealism so that we can have our romance and our sanity too, the deus ex machina in the guise of Dogberry is already descending. He is bringing with him the metaphysics of comedy, for the happiest moment we can know in this vale of tears is that sudden fantasy that the scheme of things is conspiring with our native wit to make up the world according to our wishes. If it weren't Dogberry it would be another incarnation of this god who superintends such moments. As Aristotle says, the deus ex machina is all wrong for tragedy, which depends for its effect on probability, but (although Aristotle is silent) it is just right for comedy which depends for its effect on improbability. This god, who in real life is always busy elsewhere, in comedy is always ready overhead to descend at the propitious moment. Here the particular incarnation in Dogberry and company is just right because, as Borachio says, with a touch of invidious irony to make his culpability more tolerable, "What your wisdoms could not discover these shallow fools have brought to light." Had it been prudent he might have gone further, saying that far from trying to discover, their wisdoms demonstrated a positive avidity for deception, and that once deceived, a taste for cruelty. The high comedy asses, full of the fustian of romance, are left speechless by this clown's doubletalk from the god. Low nonsense drowns out high nonsense. Claudio is next seen talking like a man of this world, fit now for a revived Hero. All he has to do is keep his mouth shut when she is unveiled.

THE GENRE OF ROMANTIC COMEDY

In this scene Beatrice takes on the manipulating habits of so many of Shakespeare's wonder women who are surrogate playwrights, getting people onstage, doing the right dialogue, winding up the peripety, in order to will down the deus ex machina. She tells Benedick a thing or two that he could not have found out by himself about the larger possibilities of their roles. And it is right that following this enlargement of their theatre and the descent of the god, the play should end with a little ritualistic masque restoring Hero the abused maiden to life and delivering Beatrice as though she were another mysterious virgin being awarded the hero to end the play. One mysterious virgin, a vision of perfection, just what the romance hero wants, is handed over. The other unveils and opens her mouth, instantly starting up another witty slanging match, now, recapitulating and humorously parodying with a new grace their smart talk of the play's opening.

> BENEDICK: Soft and fair, Friar. Which is Beatrice?
> BEATRICE (unmasks): I answer to that name. What is your
>   will?
> BENEDICK: Do not you love me?
> BEATRICE: Why no, no more than reason.
>
> . . . .
>
> BEATRICE: Do not you love me?
> BENEDICK: Troth, no, no more than reason.

Hero is the serious piece of romance, Beatrice the parodic, as usual, but now Beatrice and Benedick have incorporated the romance code in their play rather than playing against it. They are on top of their own roles as well as those of the romance figures and know what to do with them. The code of romance has its irresistible charms but is likely to do least damage in the keeping of people who have their wits about them.

If now we come back to the question of the "contamination" of the genres, we see that the fantasy of the plot proposed at the opening of this essay, Rinaldo riding at Beatrice's will from the forests of *Orlando Furioso* into domestic Messina to inhabit the figure of the joker Benedick, thus collapsing the postures of the romance, benign and malign, into the theatre of Beatrice and Benedick, does in fact figure the action of the play.

Comedy is a fantasy of triumph, giving an access of superiority, as though somehow—by wit, accident, fortune, the god's intervention—we had mastered the perverse will of contingent life to sink down into the inert or fly into incoherent bits and pieces. This instant of mastery has no future, being what is right and therefore timeless. Thus it has to be marriage (the ritual) at the end, not fornication, because the ritual is a speech act—"I take this man . . . ," "I pronounce you . . ."—magically giving for an instant a local habitation and name to the metaphysic of comedy, the fantasy that we can get on top of things and reorder the world as the god ought to have done. He is always looking the other way in real life but the metaphysic of comedy wills him to descend and do his job properly.

Beatrice and Benedick have worked their game-playing talents up into proper comedy, a futureless instant in which reason masters romance and puts to use what it has to offer. This play is not a sociological tract promoting well-adjusted marriages in which the illusion of romance is tempered by common sense. These characters have no psychological past and they have no psychological future. They have got up—invented—the instant of rightness in which the two fantasies of comedy and romance work together. We leave them dancing, to lighten, as Benedick says, their wives' heels—another of his double entendres to deliver sexuality from its romantic sublimities. No need to know more, whether the heels stayed light or whether gravity began to set in again.

For this one moment a surrogate playwright almost as clever as the original is required. Shakespeare's metaphor, "the world is a stage," is inexact. What it ought to say is that the World wants to be a stage and is looking for an accomplished playwright.

In its fantasy comedy is essentially different from realism. In the realistic novel, for example, the more realism the less perfect the closure, but comedy always has perfect closure. It would not be comedy without perfect closure, for then the improbable on which comedy battens would tend to become the probable and we would lapse into another genre. At the end of comedy all the personae have perfect identity and they know their names. Questions of identity—mistakes, masks, acting, speaking in tongues, manipulating—are always at the center of the action. At the end there are no questions of identity. Role-playing is the way to the absolute role at the end. Beatrice is many roles during the action but she is only Beatrice at the end. If brains are in short supply, there is always fortune to work things out, but the greatest joy is the alliance of brains and fortune.

Aristotle says that comedy is an imitation of actions of men who are a species of the ugly. The heavy father, miser, doctor, teacher, lawyer, braggart warrior, parasite, jealous lover, shrew, and so on, are certainly a species of the ugly. Even the wily servant or slave, brainy as he is, must be counted an ugly because he twists everything to gain his supper. He has none of the Aristotelian ethical man in him. These masks of classical comedy are spasms and contortions of the human spirit.

(Outside the puppet theatre in the Jardin de Luxembourg the leaden gendarme passes, telling the children to get off the wall, stay on the path, off the grass; inside, Guignol dances up behind the leaden gendarme. He has a maniacal grin, he is swinging his long baton with a crazy gaiety. He turns to the children to ask them whether he should crown the cop. They scream, "Yes!" Hand to his ear, hard of hearing. "Yes!" He knocks off the policeman's head. It rolls across the stage. The policeman disappears into the wings running to catch his head. Outside the gendarme passes; the children do not think of disobeying him.)

Comedy is a fantasy of triumph but the triumph of *Much Ado* and of all Shakespearean romantic comedy is rather different from anything Aristotle could have imagined. It is not that the ugly masks have disappeared. On the contrary in this play Beatrice is parodying the shrew and Benedick the braggart warrior, but they are as it were doppelgängers, gracious figures playing with comic masks. (Claudio, Leonato, Don John, Dogberry, even Hero, are more classical.) To play with the mask is not at all the same thing as to be the mask.

How did this change in comedy come about? In high comedy the central figures are not species of the ugly because they are gentlefolk, far gone in idiocy perhaps, but always capable of rediscovering their gentle nature. They have wit and style and grace and are potentially the lords and masters of their faces. Benedick metamorphoses into a rational Rinaldo and Beatrice into a worldly Ginevra because they have from the start their self-creating—or self-recreating—qualities in them. We remember Sidney's apology for romance, that it has moved men's hearts to the exercise of courtesy, liberality, and courage. These are certainly the qualities that the "Kill Claudio!" scene bestows on the witcrackers Beatrice and Benedick—or rather the qualities they bestow on themselves by assuming the roles in their own theatre. These roles are artificial, artful, something made. They gratify the desire to render life gracious. Shakespeare and Sidney are at one in this. The qualities that grace romance are the qualities that make for high comedy figures and it is romance that has given them to comedy. Shakespeare and few of his contemporaries saw the possibility of a new comedy in which masks of classical comedy would merge with the grace of romance. For this the figures must become doppelgängers.

Where Shakespeare is modern in a way that Ariosto, Sidney, and Spenser are not is in his obsession, evidenced in so many plays, that in the graciousness of romance there is inescapably hidden the corruption of violence, cruelty, and destruction. Of course these two sides of romance are present in all romances, Ariosto's, Spenser's, the modern western. What is different in Shakespeare is that the one is conceived as implicit in the other, not as two halves of a "Manichean" world. This conception, a reimagining of romance, is one frame of the plot of *Much Ado*. Another frame is its mastery by the game-playing rationalists so that they incorporate the benign and make the malign the object of ridicule. That they can do this is as much a part of the comic pleasure as that it is done. Brainy opportunism in this case is not only wit play but masking to put on the right play. They are, however, themselves victims of mistaken identity—it is a defect of their virtue as they are too fond of their powers, but Claudio is always mistaken as to his identity until Borachio's confession "runs like iron through the blood" and then he is no longer that dangerous mooncalf creature Benedick defines: "Some strange bull leapt your father's cow and got a calf." He no longer has the bleat; he is now a high-comedy figure, the gracious cavalier.

This is the fantasy of triumph of this play and of romantic comedy. In *Much Ado* the fantasy is contained in the plot of creating a rational Rinaldo and a worldly Ginevra who have control of the romance. The audience can celebrate courtesy, liberality, and courage along with native wit and the office of the god from the machine. This is high comedy and it owes everything to Shakespeare's vision of romance and his will to contaminate the genres.

Much Ado about Nothing: The Temptation to Isolate

Joseph Westlund

Unlike *The Merchant of Venice, Much Ado about Nothing* is not a seductive play; it invites us into no world of wish fulfillment, but instead seems to hold us at arm's length. *Much Ado about Nothing* "has never provoked elaborate critical appraisal"; some, like Dr. Johnson and C. L. Barber, decline to interpret it. Although Beatrice and Benedick win everyone's praise, the play as a whole seems to make critics rather uncomfortable, and yet uncertain why this should be so. For instance, Humphreys writes of the stage history: "Messina's world has not struck everyone as essentially good-natured. Yet essentially good-natured is surely what it is" (Arden edition). G. K. Hunter remarks that "the whole work is more bitter than is usually allowed; the world of Messina buys its elegance dearly; it is a world . . . where the comic vision of happiness is available only to those with enough poise to remain balanced and adaptive throughout conflict and deception." On the other hand, the relationship between Beatrice and Benedick conveys a depth of love quite new to these plays—a classic instance of reparation based on acknowledgment of guilt and a chance to repair the wrong.

Part of *Much Ado* suggests that control is good, and another part suggests that it is bad: a manipulation which deprives characters of their autonomy. We need to clarify the issue. There is so much deception that the play easily awakens fear in the characters, and in us,

From *Shakespeare's Reparative Comedies: A Psychoanalytic View of the Middle Plays.* © 1984 by the University of Chicago. University of Chicago Press, 1984.

about being small, helpless, and controlled by others. These fears live on in us from childhood; as Erik Erikson puts it:

> The unavoidable imposition on the child of outer controls which are not in sufficient accord with his inner control at the time, is apt to produce in him a cycle of anger and anxiety. This leaves a residue of an *intolerance of being manipulated* and coerced beyond the point at which outer control can be experienced as self-control.

Because Beatrice and Benedick can experience outer control—the tricks played on them—as self-control, they achieve a positive advance: they rise above their defensive isolation and convincingly fall in love before our very eyes. However, Claudio and Hero are subjected to outer controls which they can only experience as impositions: they feel pushed about, and so do we insofar as we identify with them. We may unconsciously feel discomfited by their world, and even by the play's maneuvering them into a happy solution at the end—one which, unlike Beatrice and Benedick's, robs them of autonomy because it has so little basis in their changed perception of each other or of the numerous deceits.

Messina is at once a world with too much control and too little— the worst of all possibilities since it causes confusion and anger, as well as the feeling of being manipulated. Numerous characters intrude on one another, yet the ones who ought to be in control, the protectors, are bungling. First let us glance at the endemic control. Pedro benignly fools Beatrice and Benedick; John malevolently plots against his brother by deceiving him and Claudio; the Friar ineffectually tries to make all end well by setting up a ruse about Hero's death. The play begins with a rehearsal of this consistent pattern: Pedro woos Hero for Claudio and thereby sets off a series of misunderstandings. Since everyone expects some sort of trickery, everyone's perception of reality grows warped. Such a pattern can make us feel rather like the characters: open to anxiety about being manipulated. What makes the effect more intense is that *Much Ado* lacks a central controlling figure—such as Portia, Rosalind, or Viola—under whose benign protection events turn out well. All the guardians in *Much Ado* fail to be sufficiently protective. In Shakespeare's comedies the law and its representatives usually have things firmly in hand. Here we find an intrusive prince, a hasty and ineffectual governor and father (Leonato), a bungling constable, and a rather ineffectual friar. As prince, Don Pedro might be expected to stand for paternal and social order; he means well, but continually interferes and proves disconcertingly credulous. In *All's Well,* the King turns matchmaker, like Don Pedro, but only because of a clear need: he must reward Helena and make his decision stick. Don Pedro does not come across as a ruler at all. He might be expected to speak to Hero and to her father on behalf of his courtier's desire to wed, but he goes beyond the call of duty in pretending to be Claudio and woo her in disguise. Pedro's behavior during the entire play suggests a compulsive need to intervene in others' affairs.

In this he and his brother Don John have much in common, although John intervenes for evil ends. John's friends advise him not to show his true colors until he "may do it without controlment" by Pedro (1.3.19). He bridles at finding himself in such a position:

> I am trusted with a muzzle and enfranchised with a clog; therefore I have decreed not to sing in my cage. If I had my mouth I would bite; if I had my liberty I would do my liking: in the meantime, let me be that I am, and seek not to alter me.
>
> (1.3.30–35)

Don John automatically takes even Conrade's sound advice as an attempt to infringe upon his liberty. The sentiment reverberates through the play: "Let me be that I am, and seek not to alter me." Although critics find John's character two dimensional, his slander of Hero can make sense as an attempt to control others rather than himself be subject to manipulation. John plots against Hero, just as he rebelled against his brother before the play began, because he resents and fears "controlment." This version varies from its source in a way which underscores the point: John tries to harm his brother because he has just defeated and "muzzled" him, not because of an unsuccessful love affair. The issue for John is anger at manipulation, not love. The two brothers, one good, one bad, color the world of the play so that it seems a peacetime version of the battlefield from which the men have just returned.

Like the Prince and his brother, Hero's father meddles; worse, he either undercontrols or overcontrols: he fails to protect his daughter, and later forces her slanderer to marry "another Hero." This tendency is disturbing. The Prince, Hero's father, and her suitor give no sign of being able to assume the protective role which we expect of them. Perhaps Shakespeare dropped the mysterious Innogen of the

Quarto because it would be too painful for us to watch Hero's mother also stand by idly.

It is unusual for a Shakespearean comedy that so much anger pervades the play; Don John's rage seems surprising largely because of its unvarying intensity. Pedro, Claudio, Leonato, and Antonio lapse into moments of fury; even Beatrice and Benedick seal their bond of affection with a pact to kill Claudio. When the characters feel pushed about, or feel that someone dear to them has been pushed about, they grow testy. Those who intrude, or merely seem to intrude, are regarded as wholly bad. Many characters find it impossible at one time or another to tolerate mixed feelings; instead, they split their views of one another in a defense against intolerable ambivalence. (Benedick, in contrast, can tolerate being of two minds about Claudio's guilt—unlike Beatrice—and is reluctant to pledge to kill him.) The prevalence of manipulation, anger, and splitting makes for an extraordinary sort of world for a festive comedy (and I suspect this is why C. L. Barber avoids the play). Such attitudes are largely confined to Shylock in *The Merchant*; when they flare up in *As You Like It* they do so only briefly, and are kept to a minimum in *Twelfth Night*.

II

Critics note the dissimilarity between the two love plots—what E. K. Chambers refers to as a "clashing of dramatic planes." Nevertheless, until the middle of the play when Beatrice and Benedick lower their defenses, suspicion characterizes their relationship just as much as it does Claudio and Hero's. First, let us consider Claudio's wooing, for it sets the mood in Messina. Some allege that the problems which critics find in his behavior are not there; he is not a rounded character, not psychologically consistent, and so we ought not to expect that he be (Storey). Not every Shakespearean character is psychologically consistent (as I argue elsewhere); but Claudio's behavior becomes comprehensible in the context of a world in which almost everyone expects to be manipulated, and behaves accordingly.

Even before Claudio appears we learn to expect a sentimental figure, one in whom aggression and tenderness are at odds: a young man, who during the recent war, excelled in "doing, in the figure of a lamb, the feats of a lion" (1.1.13–14). The euphuistic terms emphasize the courtly artifice which surrounds him, and prepare us for an apparently conventional emotion. When Claudio sees Hero he falls in love at first sight, but says nothing to her—nor does she say anything to him. Once she leaves, however, he interrupts Benedick's resolute and defensive banter:

CLAUDIO: Thou thinkest I am in sport: I pray thee tell me
  truly how thou lik'st her.
BENEDICK: Would you buy her, that you inquire after her?
CLAUDIO: Can the world buy such a jewel?
BENEDICK: Yea, and a case to put it into. But speak you this
  with a sad brow? . . .
CLAUDIO: In mine eye, she is the sweetest lady that ever I
  looked on.

(1.1.165–75)

Some people think his attitude businesslike. Instead, it strikes me as highly, dangerously, idealized. Hero rarely speaks, so that Claudio, and we, can imagine her as perfect: "a jewel," "the sweetest lady." Claudio seems conventional, not a hard-nosed participant in an arranged marriage, but an overly sentimental lover. As such, he exposes himself to manipulation almost at once. Don Pedro's busybody intervention nearly makes Claudio give up Hero; then Don John's slanderous intervention makes him radically degrade her.

In Freudian terms these polar responses, idealization and degradation, are defenses against anxiety caused by sexual impulses. Arthur Kirsch, following Freud, says that "the heated carnal fantasies that emerge in [Claudio's] charges against Hero suggest the repression of his own sensuality, and his idealistic interest in her tends from the start to be overly self-centered." Kirsch finds Claudio's psychology not developed, his characterization largely muted. We can better understand Claudio's character if we slightly shift the terms in a direction which Melanie Klein mapped out. Freud thought of sexual impulses as existing apart from relationships to others and love as sublimated surplus libido. Klein thought of sexuality and love as implicated from the start in relationships to "objects" (persons, or aspects of persons). As J. O. Wisdom concludes: "According to Freud, the problem [of neurosis, of guilt and anxiety] arises over sexuality imperfectly directed toward the sexual object, whereas in Melanie Klein it concerns aggressiveness ambivalently directed toward the sexual object." Klein gives more adequate emphasis to aggression in relation to sex and love.

Claudio is easier to understand from Klein's perspective, for we need not postulate "heated carnal fantasies." They are not clearly present in any of the lovers in the festive comedies. Instead, we can focus on Claudio's anger and aggression, which are overt and stirred up by his finding himself at the center of a court intrigue after having just returned from war. His "conventional" romantic sentiments result more from repressed aggression than from repressed sexuality. Claudio preserves Hero, "the sweetest lady," in an isolated state—one uncontaminated and safe from angry attacks. He idealizes her, and in doing so he denies her sexuality. When her sexuality emerges, it proves intolerable and persecutory. He feels deceived and manipulated by her. He cannot bring these splits closer together so as to conceive of Hero as a whole person, someone about whom he might have mixed feelings which he could tolerate. He seems unable to feel guilt about the aggression he directs toward her. G. K. Hunter remarks that "a relationship which, like that of Hero and Claudio, omits to notice the self-will, suspiciousness and acerbity of the individual [which Beatrice and Benedick notice] is incomplete and riding for a fall." Claudio first comes to life when he vents his rage during the church scene. Of course, sexual aggression is transformed into wit in *Much Ado,* but the continual jokes about cuckoldry indicate as much aggression as sexuality. Being cuckolded makes the man feel intensely manipulated: by the spouse, by the lover, and by the public at large. To make the joke is both an attack and a defense. Because of the brittle defensiveness which prevails at court, Claudio does not know how to take the Prince's remark about Hero: "Amen, if you love her, for the lady is very well worthy" (1.1.205). To this unambiguous and unambivalent statement, Claudio replies in the guarded way which characterizes him and Messina: "You speak this to fetch me in, my lord."

Up to this point Claudio seems about to embark upon a tender, uneventful love quest:

> war-thoughts
> Have left their places vacant, in their rooms
> Come thronging soft and delicate desires,
> All prompting me how fair young Hero is,
> Saying I lik'd her ere I went to wars.
>
> (1.1.281–85)

The complication which immediately ensues gives us our first fleeting glimpse of his vulnerability to overcontrol. Don Pedro appropriately offers to negotiate, to "break with her, and with her father, / And thou shalt have her" (1.1.289–90). He alters his plan: "I will assume thy part in some disguise, / And tell fair Hero I am Claudio, / And in her bosom I'll unclasp my heart" (1.1.301–3). Strangely, Claudio says nothing about this unnecessarily fanciful scheme. Why Pedro suggests it, and why Claudio acquiesces are inexplicable unless we refer to the pattern of manipulation.

Within twenty lines this intrusive scheme becomes secondhand and distorted news. Antonio reports that Pedro himself loves Hero (1.2.10–12). In the next scene, Borachio says that he "heard it agreed upon that the Prince should woo Hero for himself, and having obtained her, give her to Count Claudio" (1.3.57–60). But what was agreed upon was that Pedro would break with Hero and her father, and would woo her as if he were Claudio, not "woo Hero for himself." Borachio, like most of the play's eavesdroppers, hears what he expects to hear: some deception. Similarly, Antonio and Leonato readily believe what they hear. Even though John has been clearly told about Pedro's plan to give Hero to Claudio, he jumps to the conclusion that "Sure my brother is amorous on Hero" (2.1.145). He expects treachery from his brother, and hence cannot believe what his own spy has told him. Like everyone else, Benedick believes the false report. Beneath the comic confusion, and beneath the rehearsal of a pattern of good deception defeating bad deception, we glimpse a troubling world in which everyone readily suspects everyone else. Even the supposedly plain-dealing villain can trust neither the report nor his own eyes.

Characters are so isolated that they lose their basis of trust in actual and internalized relations to others. Claudio accepts the Prince's apparent deception so readily that his love seems hollow, perhaps just a businesslike wish to wed as well as possible. Yet what he says is startling:

> Let every eye negotiate for itself,
> And trust no agent; for beauty is a witch
> Against whose charms faith melteth into blood.
> (2.1.166–68)

Such acquiescence is suspect not because pallid, but because of the barely concealed rage. No wise courtier would challenge his prince, but the tone is unsettling. If Claudio will "trust no agent," why does he persist in such reliance throughout the play? He continually lets others do what he could be expected to do for himself, yet readily fears that they trick him. There is a passive-agressive quality here, and it seems a defense against the longing to trust others—and, indeed, to fuse with them (as he longs to merge with an idealized Hero). He "trusts" Pedro again, instantly believes the slander—and then the Friar's scheme, and finally Leonato's offer of another Hero. Claudio continually gets just what he expects: some deception.

I hesitate to make Claudio so complex, but the psychological consistency is there and contributes to the play's effect: he voices fear of manipulation and reveals the self-fulfilling nature of paranoia. Beatrice and Benedick, for instance, are in much the same state for a large part of the play, yet they are ready and able to stand on their own two feet. Claudio's more precarious independence results in more potent and diffuse anger. For instance, his philosophical acceptance of Don Pedro's apparent deceit is a sham; its petulance flares out when he vows to "trust no agent." Then he focuses his anger on Hero: "beauty is a witch / Against whose charm faith melteth into blood." Kirsch draws a parallel to Othello, which indicates, rightly, that the lines are far from businesslike or vapid. Claudio disturbs viewers in subterranean ways: they find him a cad, or deny that he is furious, or find him conventional (which does not get one very far). In the most thorough indication of how unsettling he is, they deny him psychological consistency. Claudio, however, is all too consistent for comfort. When Pedro ends the confusion and hands over Hero, Claudio reverts to his (by now suspicious) tenderness; he resorts to an idealization of Hero that can make us uneasy after his condemnation of beauty as a witch: "Silence is the perfectest herald of joy. . . . I give away myself for you and dote upon the exchange" (2.1.288–91).

Crime and Cover-up in Messina

Richard A. Levin

Is *Much Ado about Nothing* a disturbing comedy? The strongest evidence that it is comes in act 4, when Claudio denounces his bride-to-be at the altar for unchastity. Claudio's conduct on this occasion leaves much to be desired, and other characters also behave poorly, including Don Pedro, Claudio's friend and patron, and Leonato, father of the prospective bride. Though critics often extenuate what they regard as the momentary transgression of Leonato and Don Pedro, Claudio has not escaped so easily. Though the wedding scene exhibits him at his worst, Claudio's overall performance has attracted, as one critic remarks, "a whole thesaurus of abuse." When *Much Ado* is reckoned a disturbing play, Claudio is generally the reason.

Yet many critics accept the judgment, offered within the play, that Don John is "the author of all" the mischief that occurs and the other characters are essentially good, though of course not without minor faults or occasional departures from the path of virtue. For example, in describing the opposition between Don John and the others, one critic writes: "The theme of anti-love [is] stitched in dark contrast . . . upon the bright fabric of love, the theme of sullen negation matched against a society of love and courtesy." Another critic, however, exemplifies the recent tendency to distribute blame more evenly: "In Messina . . . we find a dark underside to human behavior, partly because we meet here . . . conscious human villainy . . . but partly

From *Love and Society in Shakespearean Comedy: A Study of Dramatic Form and Content.* © 1985 by Associated University Presses, Inc. University of Delaware Press, 1985.

also because the impulses of the villain sometimes find expression in the behavior of well-intentioned characters as well." Whether or not Messina's "well-intentioned" citizens have dubious motives depends to a great degree on the extent to which one believes dramatic conventions function to limit the search for plausible psychological motivation. For example, Don John's self-proclaimed dedication to evil perhaps marks him as a stage villain whose raison d'être is to plot against virtue. If he lacks roundedness as a character, he is less likely to be seen as a product of society and a reflection of its faults. Other dramatic conventions function directly to protect the "good" characters. Thus, when Claudio and the others readily lend credence to Don John's accusations against Hero, the play reveals not the weakness of particular characters but the devastating results of slander. Similarly, the ceremonial aspects of Claudio's dirge scene can be taken as symbolic indication that his repentance for Hero's death is more than perfunctory.

I myself am convinced that Shakespeare does allow for a reading guided by such conventions, but I think he also permits a far more rigorous assessment of the characters. That—with the exception of Claudio—Messina has commonly escaped harsh criticism reflects, I think, *Much Ado*'s dependence on social nuances—nuances that, though present in *The Merchant of Venice*, exist in that play side-by-side with starker effects.

Much Ado consists largely of upper-class conversation among friends and relatives who are at leisure to enjoy one another's company. It has often been noted that their drawing-room conversation anticipates Restoration and eighteenth-century English drama, as well as the novel as practiced, for example, by Jane Austen. It is less often noted that, like the best of his successors, in depicting such conversation, Shakespeare implies a complex set of social attitudes and social pressures. To appreciate the drama that unfolds, the audience must often respond to "impressions" gathered from the conversation, or to small gestures that suggest underlying stresses. At other times, the placid tone of conversation is broken by the more acerbic voice of Beatrice, who, in her role as *eiron*, punctures the illusions that others live by. I have already discussed [elsewhere] Beatrice's response to the announcement of her cousin's betrothal, beginning, "Good Lord, for alliance! Thus goes every one to the world but I." Beatrice identifies the social pressure exerted on all the characters who are single and of marriageable age. She thereby helps to identify the temptations they are exposed to in the course of the play. A disruption such as that which takes place at the wedding represents, in my opinion, not the intrusion of an alien force, but tensions that have gradually come to a head. One is ultimately led to question whether Messina has a right to rejoice at the end of the play. As soon as attention shifts from Don John's malevolence to the subtler social forces in Messina, everyone shares a measure of responsibility for all that happens.

When *Much Ado* opens, Leonato's invited guest, Don Pedro, prince of Arragon, is approaching Messina, and he has sent a messenger ahead with a letter:

> LEONATO: How many gentlemen have you lost in this action?
> MESSENGER: But few of any sort, and none of name.
> LEONATO: A victory is twice itself when the achiever
>   brings home full numbers. I find here that Don Pedro
>   hath bestow'd much honor on a young Florentine
>   call'd Claudio.
>
>   (1.1.5–11)

This brief interchange illustrates the kind of interpretive problem *Much Ado* often poses. In these first few lines, at least, the audience strongly inclines towards taking at face value the report of a great victory. However, so little is said about the battle that no one can be sure what did happen, and a few of the details leave open other possibilities. Few men were killed, one assumes, because the soldiers fought well—not because they engaged in a negligible skirmish. And presumably "none of name" died because the nobility fought valiantly—not because the nobility avoided its responsibility to lead troops into battle. No explanation of the military action preceding the opening of the play is ever forthcoming, and perhaps Leonato's unconcern should be ours; yet Beatrice seems to comment on his omission when she raises sceptical questions about the battle.

In paraphrasing the messenger, Leonato makes an outright error when he speaks of a victory with "full numbers" (overlooking the losses among the lower sort), or else his words are supposed to be taken as gnomic wisdom—but even then application of his proverbial saying would mean that he counts the losses of the lower sort as insignificant. Leonato's attention then turns to news of Claudio. The written text does not make clear why Claudio is significant to him, but in view of the flirtation that has already gone on between Claudio and Hero (1.1.296–300), it may be that Leonato reads with a wink for his daughter; he has marriage in mind for her. Why is Don Pedro writing that he has "bestow'd much honor" on Claudio? In thus honoring

Claudio, has Don Pedro sought to please Leonato? Leonato asks for no explanations. (The Elizabethans might have thought of what Lawrence Stone calls "the inflation of honors," the military knighthoods Essex conferred, for example.) The messenger (in a passage not quoted) starts to elaborate, but his language is so flowery that nothing can be gathered from it; he even seems to mock Leonato's lack of curiosity by concluding that Claudio "hath indeed better bett'red expectation than you must expect of me to tell you how" (ll. 15–17). Leonato does not pursue the subject and he soon makes a remark that helps to expose him as a complacent man, not eager to make more than superficial judgments. Upon hearing from the messenger that Claudio's uncle wept upon getting news of his nephew's safe return, Leonato comments: "There are no faces truer than those that are . . . wash'd" with tears (ll. 26–27). Leonato's trust in tears is a detail Shakespeare will draw on later (4.1.154).

Beatrice now interjects herself, as if dissatisfied with the desultory pace of the conversation. Her uncle has taken care to note Claudio's survival; she wants to know whether Benedick, the man who interests her, has returned. Her manner of questioning sets her apart from her uncle, however; she asks the messenger penetrating questions, probes him about what Benedick has achieved—and not achieved—in battle. She is openly dubious about his accomplishments. She concludes, for example, that his "good service . . . in these wars" consists of his having helped to eat "musty victual." Nor is Beatrice merely a gadfly; her questions, she implies, arise from her own uncomfortable experiences with Benedick; she questions not only his bravery and his intelligence, but his capacity for friendship: "He wears his faith but as the fashion of his hat: it ever changes with the next block" (ll. 75–77). Beatrice has well-developed suspicions about Benedick's nature and implies that she will take no husband who does not meet high standards. Nevertheless, in bringing Benedick into the conversation, Beatrice perhaps wishes to indicate that she, like her cousin, may marry some day. She is certainly put under pressure to conform. Leonato quickly disparages her independence. Benedick will "be meet with you," he reminds her, and then he chides her about her professed imperviousness to love: "You will never run mad, niece." "No, not till a hot January," is Beatrice's robust reply, but later she may compromise her standards.

Though just a few lines into the play, currents beneath the surface of conversation are becoming evident. Ostensibly Leonato and his family have merely undertaken to entertain guests. Actually, everyone waits expectantly for the arrival of bachelors and for the beginning of a time for courtship.

Upon entering, Don Pedro greets his host: "Good Signior Leonato, are you come to meet your trouble? The fashion of the world is to avoid cost, and you encounter it" (ll. 96–98). Is Don Pedro grateful for Leonato's "trouble," or is he observing Leonato's excessive hospitality, the care haute bourgeoisie takes with aristocracy? Later Don Pedro calls himself a "charge," and he responds to Leonato's wish that his stay will be a long one by saying, "I dare swear [Leonato] is no hypocrite" (l. 151)—insisting a little too much, so it seems, that Leonato has no ulterior motive. Don Pedro apparently mistrusts Leonato's courtesy.

A few details suggest that Don Pedro's discomfort has something to do with the expectation that courting will follow his arrival. Although he has visited frequently, he seems not to recognize Leonato's daughter, and he recovers himself only to offer an awkward compliment, likening Hero's appearance to her father's (ll. 104, 111–12). Don Pedro's subsequent response suggests a stage direction; his attention is on Claudio, whose eyes are on Hero. As Don Pedro exits with Leonato, he still watches Claudio and notices him staying behind and beckoning Benedick to join him. As quickly as Don Pedro can, he extricates himself and goes to seek Claudio and to inquire after his "secret" (1.1.202–4). Evidently he guesses that Claudio is inclined to marry.

I believe we gradually come to entertain a hypothesis about Don Pedro. Born and bred a prince, elegant in dress and manner, he seems to embody the social values held dear in Messina. Yet he has never married, though he is possibly somewhat beyond the age at which most men do. Knowing that he will never court and knowing, nevertheless, that all thoughts in Messina will turn to marriage, he brings with him, as a well-trained guest, valuable presents—two eminently eligible bachelors, on one of whom, a count, he has newly bestowed "honor." Don Pedro seems eager to adapt himself to conventional life—indeed, is eager to promote conventional values. Nevertheless, no man is selfless; in exchange he will ask that his efforts to help others be appreciated. Leonato's overeager reception already disturbs him. Don Pedro's affection for Claudio will pose another challenge.

Before Don Pedro reenters, Claudio discloses his interest in Hero to Benedick. Claudio is sensitive to the expectations of the society around him. He has learned that when a soldier is home from the war, it is time to fall in love. He also knows that Hero is the right kind of girl for him—well-born, pretty, and wealthy. Only one more question needs to be answered, and he asks it of Benedick immediately: "Is she not a modest young lady?" (l. 165). Claudio wants to make certain that his marriage will be an asset and not a hindrance. His reasons for wanting to marry, and the promptness of his decision, show him as a rather conventional young man, without any special depth or complication of character.

Though Don Pedro anticipated a time of courtship, he is overtaken by the speed of events. He enters to discover that not only has Claudio already confessed his love, but he has chosen Benedick, not the prince, as his confidant. When Don Pedro asks to hear Claudio's "secret," Benedick, taunting Claudio, quickly discloses it. Claudio equivocates: he loves Hero "if [his] passion change not shortly" (l. 219). Don Pedro immediately senses Claudio's timidity and reassures him; "The lady is very well worthy." "You speak this to fetch me in," Claudio responds, but Don Pedro reaffirms his opinion. In supporting Claudio, Don Pedro fulfills the role he set for himself. On the other hand, Don Pedro has acquired information that at some point could be used destructively: Claudio mistrusts his own judgment, and is very much concerned to find a wife highly regarded by others.

Don Pedro wants to be alone with Claudio. However, Benedick will not leave; quite the contrary, he makes peacock display of himself, boasting that he will "live a bachelor." Don Pedro, quickly irritated, tells Benedick that he will soon "look pale with love" (l. 247). The prince implies that Benedick is only posing as a "tyrant" to the female sex; behind the mask lies a man almost as ready for marriage as Claudio. Whether Don Pedro is right or not is still unknown. However, his own resentment suggests that for him bachelorhood is painful in a way it is not for Benedick. Don Pedro's greater vulnerability—as courting gets underway—soon becomes more apparent. After trying politely to draw the conversation to a halt, he invents an errand for Claudio. Irritated, Benedick leaves with a parting retort. Using a metaphor from dressmaking, he says that Don Pedro's discourse is ornamented with loosely attached trimmings that may come off to reveal his real concerns (ll. 285–89). Benedick hints at the deceptiveness of Don Pedro's elegant surface.

As soon as Don Pedro and Claudio are alone, the latter turns for help, as Don Pedro apparently hoped he would:

CLAUDIO: My liege, your Highness now may do me good.
DON PEDRO: My love is thine; teach it but how,
　　And thou shalt see how apt it is to learn
　　Any hard lesson that may do thee good.

(1.1.290–93)

While Claudio addresses Don Pedro as a prince who is in a position to do him a favor, Don Pedro answers affectionately. He says that his "love" stands ready to learn any "hard lesson" Claudio asks of him. As the nature of Claudio's request is already obvious, Don Pedro comes very close to saying that he will find it distressful to help Claudio to a wife. Don Pedro's words are rarely, if ever, regarded as intimate, and it is true that the word *love* is common between male friends in the Renaissance. In context, however, "love" at least hints at an unusually strong emotion that Claudio does not reciprocate. In Elizabethan English, "apt" sometimes means "apt for love" and not simply "ready" or "prepared"; Don Pedro rather than expressing his passion directly, will sublimate it in an act of sacrifice for Claudio.

Don Pedro is still very much a mystery at this point in the play because, unlike Claudio, his relationship to established social patterns is undefined. His deliberate disclosure of affection for Claudio, which he could easily have avoided making, invites speculation about his motives. If he is not simply candid, he may be manipulative, either attempting to discourage Claudio from marrying, or, far more likely, thinking to strengthen their attachment so that Claudio's subsequent marriage will impose less of a separation. I am suggesting a possible parallel with *The Merchant of Venice*. When Bassanio asks his older friend, Antonio, for the money that will allow him to woo Portia, Antonio expresses his "love" for Bassanio and promises to do his "uttermost" to raise the money. Later, in Bassanio's presence, he readily agrees to the ominous terms of Shylock's loan. Both older men cannot resist accommodating their younger friends in the hope that gratitude will help strengthen the relationship.

Claudio not only fails to reciprocate; he disingenuously avoids acknowledging anything of what Don Pedro has implied. He wants nothing to divert him from the matter at hand: "Hath Leonato any son, my lord?" Critics have debated whether Claudio's inquiry into the financial side of marriage is appropriate. Shakespeare seems to me to go to some lengths to show Claudio's interest as excessive. He wants to learn about more than Hero's dowry; what will she inherit?

he asks. Like Claudio's earlier inquiry concerning Hero's "modesty," he reveals here the desire for a socially advantageous marriage. A little voice speaks to Claudio, "prompting" him, telling him that when war ends, it is time for love: "war-thoughts" are gone, he says, and "in their rooms / Come thronging soft and delicate desires" (1.1.302–3). Claudio's is not the language of authentic passion—he is not "apt," to use Don Pedro's word. The voice Claudio hears is society's, encouraging him to fall in love and marry.

Another way to judge Claudio is through Don Pedro's eyes. Don Pedro sees that Claudio prepares to gather for himself all that society can offer. Don Pedro knows what voice Claudio listens to, and finally says to him: "Thou wilt be like a lover presently, / And tire the hearer with a book of words" (ll. 306–7). The words flow too freely to be Claudio's; he has been reading from the "book" left open for young men when they return from war (cf. l. 311). Don Pedro has a right to be irritated, and therefore his offer is all the more commendable: he will speak to Leonato on Claudio's behalf.

Claudio, however, resumes the "treatise" he had begun to tell. "How sweetly you do minister to love," he tells Don Pedro, imagining him as the idealized older patron of romance. At this point, Don Pedro's mood shifts. He breaks in with: "What need the bridge much broader than the flood?"—that is, Claudio's is a familiar human need that does not warrant excessive fuss. Then Don Pedro, without explanation, substitutes a new and far less straightforward scheme for helping Claudio to his bride.

At a masked dance that evening, Don Pedro will disguise himself as Claudio and woo Hero for him. The change in plan invites close scrutiny. Don Pedro is perhaps conscious of three motives. He will help his young friend. He will encourage in him a feeling of gratitude. And third, he will find for himself a role on an occasion when his own failure to woo would otherwise be noticeable. But does the plot also show Don Pedro unconsciously finding a channel for destructive emotion, were he to wish to release it? He goes so far as to imply that were he not wooing for Claudio, he might have an interest of his own in her: in Hero's "bosom I'll unclasp my heart, / And take her hearing prisoner with the force / And strong encounter of my amorous tale" (ll. 323–25). He could make Claudio jealous, if he chose. The scheme will also keep Claudio and Hero apart, thus preventing a firm relationship from growing up between them.

I have argued that to understand all the action seen so far one needs to recognize that the time to marry has arrived in Messina. Claudio responds to the pressure very directly; Benedick less directly; Don Pedro most indirectly of all. So far, only slight signs have appeared that the strain will overwhelm anyone.

Having watched how social forces influence others, we are prepared to see them at work in Don John, who is now introduced. He announces at once: "I cannot hide what I am" (1.3.13); then he declares himself "a plain-dealing villain" (l. 32). For some critics, a self-revelation this emphatic settles the matter: Don John is a pure figure of evil, "a thing of darkness out of step with his society," who "hates the children of light simply because they generate radiance in a world he prefers to see dark." If this description is correct, then *Much Ado* approaches melodrama by artificially dividing the good from the bad characters. I believe, on the other hand, that Don John should not divert us from the evil within society, and to make this point, Shakespeare shows that Don John is shaped by the same social forces that mould others.

When he announces himself a villain, he is not alone—he speaks to Conrade—and by this time in the play one looks beneath the surface of drawing-room chatter. Even Don John's handling of language shows him to be as conscious of himself as a social being as anyone in the play. He makes elegant use of balance and antithesis—in the following sentence, for example: "I am trusted with a muzzle, and enfranchis'd with a clog, therefore I have decreed not to sing in my cage" (ll. 32–34). Certain inferences may be drawn from the things Don John does tell Conrade, and more information is forthcoming.

Conrade opened the scene by asking Don John, "Why are you thus out of measure sad?" Don John answers evasively by referring only to "the occasion." Context, however, defines the "occasion" as the same one that distresses Don Pedro—Leonato's preparations for an evening of dance and courtship. This explanation is soon confirmed. When Borachio, another member of Don John's retinue, enters, he tells Don John that he comes with news "of an intended marriage." Don John replies: "What is he for a fool that betroths himself to unquietness?" Here is a statement with strong feeling behind it!

Although the play terms them "brothers" and both enjoy the rank of prince, Don John is apparently a bastard and he and Don Pedro half brothers. Each surrounds himself with two male followers: Don John with Conrade and Borachio, and Don Pedro with Claudio and Benedick. Alliteration, syllabication, and accentuation connect the two groups of names. Like Don Pedro. Don John is distinguished from his retinue by his lack of interest in courting a woman. While Benedick and Claudio woo, Borachio resumes a liaison with Margaret. When Beatrice remark that Don Pedro does not make himself available to women, she links the two brothers: "Your father got excellent husbands, if a maid could come by them" (2.1.324–25).

In analogues and sources for *Much Ado,* two friends are in love with the same woman, and the Don John figure plots to separate his friend from the lady and so obtain her for himself. Don John, of course, has no such motive. He offers as many motives as Iago does, and it is probably as treacherous to choose among them; about all we can say for sure is that he lives in a world of men and focuses his resentment on them. To speculate a little further, however, Don John and Don Pedro both focus their attentions on Claudio, though Don John's emotions are hostile while his brother's are not. Don John initially welcomes the opportunity to contrive against "that young start-up [who] hath all the glory of [his] overthrow" (1.3.66–67). Later, Don John works to drive a wedge between Claudio and his royal patron. At the end of the dance, Don John, recognizing the masked Claudio, informs him that Don Pedro has wooed for himself (2.1.164). Later, when Don John enters to report Hero's "disloyalty," he contrasts his brother's effort to effect the marriage with his own effort to protect Claudio (3.2.95–100). Whether Don John is a bidder for Claudio's affections or simply the young man's enemy is not easy to say.

In many accounts of *Much Ado,* Don Pedro and Don John are held to be of opposing natures, even if they superficially share certain traits, such as a love of intrigue. G. K. Hunter, for example, contrasts the "blind self-interest of Don John" with the "social expertise of Don Pedro." Robert G. Hunter says bluntly: "Don Pedro's function is to create love. Don John's is to destroy it." I am suggesting instead that the "melodramatic" distinction between the brothers becomes blurred, so that we are prepared to see some of Don John's ill will in his brother. One villain is not merely substituted for another, however, because Don Pedro, unlike his brother, is woven into a complex social pattern; his complicity makes the problem of guilt in the play far subtler than it seemed when Don John first announced his villainy.

Act 2 opens after the dinner with Beatrice holding forth about marriage. Her society, of course, believes strongly in marriage; she asserts contrary views:

BEATRICE: I will even take sixpence in earnest of the berrord
    [bearward, animal keeper], and lead his apes into hell.
LEONATO: Well then, go you into hell.
BEATRICE: No, but to the gate, and there will the devil meet
    me like an old cuckold with horns on his head, and
    say, "Get you to heaven, Beatrice, get you to heaven,
    here's no place for you maids."

                            (2.1.39–46)

Proverbially, old maids lead apes to hell, while mothers, led by their
children, go to heaven. Beatrice, however, places the married folk in
hell, presumably because of their misery and because they sin, not only
in taking lovers, but in marrying when they ought not to. Beatrice,
who never talks idly, is wondering about her own predicament and
Hero's, and she raises a question for the audience to keep in mind: are
the marriages in *Much Ado* well-advised?

Beatrice's feelings about marriage are more complicated than she
admits. After all, she is very much a part of Leonato's household,
which she amuses with her clever remarks. Also, it soon becomes
apparent that she has introduced Benedick and marriage into the conversation because Hero's prospects are already a subject of discussion.
Beatrice, as at the opening of the play, asserts her own romantic
interest, albeit in an indirect manner. She evidently feels the same
pressure to marry that the other single people feel.

It is greatly to Beatrice's credit that she does not try to discourage
her cousin, though Hero seems destined to go to the altar first. Overheard conversation has led Leonato to conclude that Don Pedro plans
to woo Hero in the evening, and Leonato instructs his daughter to be
ready. With a generosity Benedick has not shown Claudio in comparable circumstances, Beatrice simply cautions Hero against undue haste
(ll. 69–80). In these and other circumstances, Beatrice emerges as a
person of stature.

The dance and its aftermath prefigure later events, although the
potential for trouble is not yet realized. At the dance, others conclude
that Don Pedro courts on his own behalf, and the few overheard
words make us wonder whether he encourages the misapprehension.
When he begins to dance with Hero, he alludes to his real identity,
beneath the mask: "Within the house is Jove" (2.1.97), then he whispers: "Speak low if you speak love." While Claudio apparently suspects Don Pedro because of what Don John tells him, Benedick forms

suspicions on his own. When he alludes to them, Don Pedro studiously avoids understanding him, and then denies the allegations and throws Benedick on the defensive about another matter, his insulting behaviour to Beatrice. Shortly afterwards, Don Pedro carefully vindicates himself before the assembled household: "Here, Claudio, I have woo'd in thy name, and fair Hero is won" (ll. 298–99). He seems relieved to prove himself loyal to Claudio, as if the doubts others form about his motives make him doubt them too.

Claudio, for his part, acts inexcusably. Unlike Benedick, Claudio knew beforehand that Don Pedro danced with Hero so that he could woo her for him. Yet Claudio quickly succumbs to Don John's ploy and loses faith in his friend. Claudio replaces one romantic story with another; now "beauty is a witch / Against whose charms faith melteth into blood" (2.1.179–80). Claudio's real feelings are revealed when he says, "let every eye negotiate for itself, / And trust no agent" (ll. 178–79). As one critic remarks, Claudio feels "duped in a bargain." He appreciates neither Don Pedro nor Hero, whose loss disturbs him only as it affects his self-respect.

When Beatrice and Benedick begin to dance with one another, she may well be ready to be courted, but instead, Benedick insults her. Benedick is masked; Beatrice, possibly, is not. Benedick, believing himself undetected, takes advantage of the opportunity to trim Beatrice's sails, telling her that he has heard that she "was disdainful" and "had [her] good wit out of the 'Hundred Merry Tales' " (2.1.129–30). Beatrice's intelligence and humor are too much for Benedick's male pride, and she takes offense, as well she should. Beatrice, who does recognize Benedick beneath his mask, describes him as "the Prince's jester, a very dull fool," and says that his only "gift is in devising impossible slanders." This criticism of Benedick is especially telling because it describes Benedick as he behaves with her at this moment.

Because a question has arisen about Benedick's merit, special importance is to be attached to the following interchange between Benedick and Beatrice as the music resumes and they begin to dance:

> BEATRICE: We must follow the leaders.
> BENEDICK: In every good thing.
> BEATRICE: Nay, if they lead to any ill, I will leave them at
> the next turning.

> (2.1.150–54)

This dialogue is symbolic. Both Beatrice and Benedick set themselves up as superior to the others around them—they will make independent moral judgments and not simply "follow the leaders." Only time can determine whether they are as good as their word.

After the dance, both have an opportunity to take out their hurt on others. Benedick does so. Believing that Don Pedro has wooed for himself, Benedick seeks out Claudio and taunts him. Ironically, he sees Claudio's vulnerability but not his own: "Alas, poor hurt fowl, now will [Claudio] creep into sedges. But that my Lady Beatrice should know me, and not know me!" (2.1.202–4). Nor is Benedick through. When Don Pedro enters looking for Claudio, Benedick admonishes the prince for betraying his friend. Then, rebuked for insulting Beatrice, he can only see how she has "misus'd [him] past the endurance of a block." When she enters, he pretends not to notice her, and calls her a "harpy" (l. 271).

Beatrice acquits herself better. Speaking privately with Don Pedro, she is remarkably candid. She admits that she had once given Benedick her heart, but he betrayed her (2.1.278–82). Then she indicates that she has come to a decision; she will not be "the mother of fools" (l. 286)—that is, she no longer wants to marry Benedick. Realizing that her feelings have been hurt, the viewer does not know whether to believe her, but her judgment may be sound—she might be wise to sit out this dance and wait for another suitor.

Beatrice acts even more commendably when Claudio enters and, in the presence of everyone, Don Pedro announces that "fair Hero is won." Claudio is silent, and Beatrice prompts him: "Speak, Count, 'tis your cue" (l. 305). She understands that although Claudio has chosen to take part in a play, his moment has come and he has nothing to say. Like Claudio, Hero also lacks words—each lacks sufficient knowledge of the other. Beatrice wittily but generously gives Hero her part: "Speak, cousin, or (if you cannot) stop his mouth with a kiss." Beatrice tries to live through the happiness of Claudio and Hero.

Only when Claudio greets Beatrice as his "cousin" does she reveal her real feelings. Though she is witty, her exclamation, "Good Lord, for alliance!" is heartfelt. She knows that society exerts pressure from which she is not immune. Therefore her resolve not to marry Benedick may weaken.

Beatrice is not the only observer deeply affected by the engagement of Hero and Claudio. Don Pedro has been silent. He watches Beatrice admiringly and sympathizes with her—up to a point. Suddenly he responds to her wish for "alliance" by saying, "Lady

Beatrice, I will get you one [a husband]." His impulse is in part a generous one, but his tone is complex. With the verb "get," which is crude, and the impersonal "one," Don Pedro indicates that Beatrice's need is a common one and may be met readily. He hints that despite her pretensions, Beatrice is willing to conform.

Beatrice replies to Don Pedro with intelligence as well as wit:

> I would rather have one [a husband] of your father's getting.
> Hath your Grace ne'er a brother like you? Your father got
> excellent husbands, if a maid come by them.
>
> (2.1.322–25)

Beatrice pays Don Pedro a compliment that she knows he will value. She says that he is attractive to women, and but for his high birth, she herself would aspire to marriage with him. On the other hand, by repeating Don Pedro's equivocal words, "get" and "one," Beatrice calls attention to them and to his enigmatic role as a matchmaker. Then she raises an implicit question; why is Don Pedro never available to women, never a suitor in his own right?

Don Pedro escapes with exceptionally clever repartee. He offers himself in marriage: "Will you have me, lady?" I do not think this proposal sincere. Beatrice and Don Pedro are engaged in witty dialogue. Don Pedro well knows that the others present regard Beatrice and Benedick as a likely match, and he would not again invite the suspicion that he lets his own interests intrude. He expects his audience to see that he has set himself before the finicky Beatrice, inviting her to refuse in a clever fashion. Of course, Don Pedro also wants his proposal to suggest to others that were he not so generous, he might well seek Beatrice's hand for himself.

As is her custom, Beatrice refuses to be merely clever in her reply:

> No [she declines the prince], unless I might have another
> [husband] for working-days. Your Grace is too costly to
> wear every day. But I beseech your Grace pardon me, I was
> born to speak all mirth and no matter.
>
> (2.1.327–30)

Interpreted in one way, the remark is complimentary. Beatrice pictures the prince as he likes to see himself, set apart by his special elegance, "too costly to wear every day." But Beatrice's words also suggest that Don Pedro is permanently excluded from the "alliance" of marriage. She describes herself and the prince as well-matched for Sundays—

both superior souls, both alone—but not as suitable life companions, because an invisible but seemingly uncrossable line separates them. This line may be the one that separates the heterosexually inclined from the homosexually, but such terminology is too coarse for Shakespeare's delicate and perhaps evasive portrayal.

The moment is a poignant one. Beatrice and Don Pedro had seemed for a moment to enjoy an intimacy; then decisive differences emerge. After their interchange, each is again left alone to deal with relentless social pressures.

Beatrice, realizing that she has been indiscreet, hastily apologizes. Though the prince graciously reassures her, his reaction is soon seen to be complicated. When Leonato saves Beatrice further embarrassment by sending her on an errand, Don Pedro alludes to a new scheme, designed to bring Beatrice and Benedick together. Both schemes divert attention from Don Pedro's own failure to woo. But are in part the product of generous impulses, the first towards Claudio, the second towards Beatrice, who will be helped to the happiness denied Don Pedro himself. However, Don Pedro's introduction of both schemes comes accompanied by language denigrating romance; if Beatrice and Benedick can be brought into a "mountain of affection," then, Don Pedro assures his listeners, "Cupid is no longer an archer; his glory shall be ours, for we are the only love-gods" (ll. 385–86). Don Pedro's wit should not conceal that "love-gods" have dangerous powers. Don Pedro's scheme will create a precarious situation. Beatrice will be led to think Benedick loves her, and Benedick to think Beatrice loves him. The product of a lie, their courtship may easily be disturbed. Even as the scheme gets put into motion, it will create another danger. Like the earlier scheme, it keeps Claudio and Hero apart (Beatrice will overhear the women, and Benedick the men). Claudio, therefore, will be at Don Pedro's side when the prince demonstrates that love is only an illusion.

Having considered Don Pedro's motives for proposing the scheme, we can return to the question of why it is received so enthusiastically by his audience. Leonato does not seem to understand that "melancholy" lies beneath Beatrice's "merry" surface (ll. 341–46), so his participation in the scheme is not entirely to be explained by his interest in her well-being. Indeed, he delights to think how soon Beatrice and Benedick would be bickering: "If they were but a week married, they would talk themselves mad" (ll. 353–54). It is Don Pedro's satiric description of Benedick and Beatrice brought into a "mountain of affection" that brings Leonato to life: "My lord, I am for

you, though it costs me ten nights' watchings." Claudio quickly
provides an echo: "And I, my lord." Hero chimes in: "I will do any
modest office, my lord, to help my cousin to a good husband." Her
earnestness betrays the real motive of the three of them. Beatrice and
Benedick are aloof and superior; the conventional world wants to
bring them within its orbit.

The prosecution of the scheme helps confirm this inference. When
Benedick overhears their conversation, the men take advantage of the
opportunity to deflate his pretensions. Hero's remarks, overheard by
Beatrice, are even more illuminating. Hero criticizes Beatrice, who is
"odd, and from all fashions" (3.1.72), and "turns . . . every man the
wrong side out, / and never gives to truth and virtue that / Which
simpleness and merit purchaseth" (ll. 68–70). Shakespeare wittily
gives Hero a chance to praise "simpleness." Though in her father's
own household, she has been eclipsed by her cousin and she does
not like it. Beatrice is far more generous with her than she is with
Beatrice.

In quick succession, Beatrice and Benedick overhear that they are
loved and declare in soliloquy not only their love for one another but
their desire to marry. Beatrice and Benedick are therefore not indifferent to what others say about them and to the pressure to conform—the
contrast between Beatrice and Benedick on the one hand and Hero and
Claudio on the other gradually comes to seem less sharp. Many critics
nevertheless do tend to maintain the distinction, arguing that while
Hero and Claudio become engaged only because to do so is expected
of them, Beatrice and Benedick are well matched and merely need a
slight push toward marriage. By giving them names that alliterate,
Shakespeare has certainly invited us to think of Beatrice and Benedick
as a pair. They also have certain traits in common. Both, for example,
hold themselves aloof from society and by means of verbal wit display
a sense of superiority. Beatrice and Benedick are also undoubtedly
attracted to one another, and they spar together in order to disguise
affection, as Leonato implies: "There is a kind of merry war betwixt
Signior Benedick and [Beatrice]; they never meet but there's a skirmish
of wit between them" (1.1.61–64). Leonato nevertheless underestimates
the importance of the tension in their relationship.

The distance Beatrice and Benedick maintain allows each of them
to examine what he or she finds disturbing in the other. Beatrice's
doubts arise from questions about Benedick's moral character. I have
already mentioned one among several somewhat obscure allusions to a

past incident or incidents; Benedick apparently betrayed the intimacy that had grown up between Beatrice and himself (in addition to 2.1.278–82, see 1.1.39–42, 120–23, and 144–45). Such suspicions about Benedick are supported by his reputation as a ladies' man (see, e.g., 1.1.109–10). This trait, on which Benedick prides himself, helps to explain the reservations he has about Beatrice: she withholds admiration. Benedick complains to her: "It is certain I am lov'd of all ladies, only you excepted" (1.1.124–25). At the dance, he criticizes her "wit"; Benedick would like a wife as intelligent and as attractive as Beatrice, but he would like her to defer to him.

The problems in their relationship point to important differences between their characters. Only Beatrice is a genuine critic of society— Benedick's satirical remarks are often made to get attention; only Beatrice has self-knowledge—Benedick denies his susceptibility to social pressure; and only Beatrice is generous—Benedick resents the successes of others, as when he taunts Claudio after Claudio discloses his interest in Hero. Beatrice's greater worth is subtly caught in the contrast between their soliloquies after they are trapped.

When Claudio and Hero became engaged, Beatrice frankly admitted her loneliness. After she eavesdrops and learns how others criticize her and how Benedick loves her, her response is put in ten succinct lines (of verse). She rebukes herself sharply: "Contempt, farewell, and maiden pride, adieu!" (3.1.109). And she promises to turn over a new leaf—she will "tam[e her] wild heart to [Benedick's] loving hand" (l. 112). Were Beatrice not so desirous of marrying, she might be less inclined to accept hearsay evidence and she might hesitate to subordinate herself to Benedick. Though her new humility has its attractive side, she is perhaps too eager to sacrifice the moral independence she has held dear; Shakespeare, we note, has Beatrice express herself in rhyme of rather pedestrian character, not up to her usual standards.

Benedick soliloquizes both before and after eavesdropping. The first speech shows that, unlike Beatrice, he has not admitted to himself his desire for marriage. He portrays himself as a satisfied bachelor who will not stir himself until he finds the perfect woman (2.3.26–35). Benedick protests too strongly. Ever since Claudio disclosed his desire to marry and Benedick responded by claiming that Hero's beauty was exceeded by Beatrice's (1.1.190–92), Benedick has been keeping a careful eye on his friend's advance to the altar. Benedick describes him as "Monsieur Love" (2.3.36) and criticizes his clothes and affected speech (ll. 15–21). "May I be so converted?" he wonders (l. 22), inadvertently revealing his wish to imitate Claudio.

Benedick's second soliloquy is an important guide to the man who emerges in the latter part of the play. Unlike Beatrice, he has no suspicions whatever, though he has more reason than Beatrice to suspect treachery, for Don Pedro has promised to see him "look pale with love." Benedick believes what he hears because he wants to marry. He quickly concludes that if she loves him, her love "must be requited" (2.3.224). In other words, he has a moral obligation to her. As the speech develops, Benedick elaborates on the righteousness of his change of course. His need to justify himself is explained by his fear—"they say I will bear myself proudly" (2.3.225). And he does bear himself proudly; quite unlike Beatrice, Benedick is brimming with pride when he learns he is loved. Benedick also worries because he has loudly vaunted his independence. He begins to work out his defense: "Happy are they that hear their detractions, and can put them to mending." This has the desired moral ring, but is not quite splendid enough. "Doth not the appetite alter," he now suggests, as if he were a philosopher of human nature. Finally, he reaches for the grand: "The world must be peopled." Critics have occasionally quoted these lines out of context and made them the moral of the play. But Benedick has really trailed off into banal sophistry—"When I said I would die a bachelor, I did not think I should live till I were married."

Having wrapped himself in a moral cloak, he is ready to adopt the utterly conventional role of the lover. At least one earlier critic likened him to Malvolio, for in his next appearance, he cuts a ridiculous figure, newly shaven, absurdly dressed, and perfumed. Like Malvolio, he fails to appreciate the joke on himself. In spite of Benedick's pretensions, he is proving himself an ordinary young man.

So far I have discussed social pressures in Messina and the urge characters have to conform and make others conform. On the other hand, no decisive test has yet arisen. One may entertain doubts about a character, but one cannot clearly fault anybody. Don Pedro, the most vulnerable character, also happens to be critically placed to influence events, for he is respected by everyone. Until a day before the marriage, the good in him prevails, a situation symbolized by the control he imposes over Don John. Now, with Claudio's marriage imminent, Don Pedro begins to break.

When Don Pedro arrived in Messina, he promised a stay of "at the least a month" (1.1.149). Act 3, scene 2 opens with Don Pedro announcing a change in plans:

> DON PEDRO: I do but stay till your marriage be consummate, and then go I toward Arragon.
> CLAUDIO: I'll bring you thither, my lord, if you'll vouchsafe me.
> DON PEDRO: Nay, that would be as great a soil in the new gloss of your marriage as to show a child his new coat and forbid him to wear it.

The desire to leave Messina merely testifies to Don Pedro's growing discomfort. However, his decision to communicate his plans to Claudio represents an important weakening of his resolve to do well by Claudio. A first inclination may be to say that Don Pedro merely wishes to remind Claudio, in the words of a famous sonnet, "to love that well, which thou must leave ere long." While this is presumably Don Pedro's only conscious purpose, his apparently simple statement probes for the answer to two questions. By indicating that he will leave on Claudio's marriage day, Don Pedro asks whether his friend realizes that marriage alters all of a man's previous relationships, *even* his relationship to a patron. In choosing the verb "consummate," Don Pedro asks whether Claudio keenly anticipates the joys of the marriage bed. Claudio's disingenuous offer to accompany Don Pedro after the wedding ceremony answers both of the prince's questions—Claudio does fear losing a patron and the sexual allusion makes him uneasy.

Don Pedro thinks to respond with harmless and traditional kidding of the prospective groom. Actually, he addresses not only Claudio's sexual embarrassment, but his fears about the future. Don Pedro says that to the betrothed, marriage wears a "gloss." By leaving Messina, Claudio would "soil" this gloss. In advising him against leaving, Don Pedro implies that marriage loses its "gloss" soon enough anyway. There is a comparable implication in Don Pedro's words when he goes on to compare Claudio's anticipation of marriage and its sexual pleasures with the anticipation a child has for a new coat that gains more than its intrinsic value by being withheld. Simply to compare Claudio's emotions to a child's is to undermine his sense that marriage is a mark of maturity. To compare Claudio to a child awaiting a new coat that will soon become an old coat is to make him wonder whether his judgment is sound. In due course, Don Pedro implies, Claudio will discover the "soil" on his marriage—but by then, he may have lost what he once he had for a certainty, Don Pedro's patronage.

Apparently sensing that he is headed in a dangerous direction, Don Pedro suddenly breaks off. He decides to tease Benedick, who has swallowed the bait laid for him and now stands before them dressed in the latest fashion and an image of vanity. Inevitably—because Don Pedro has a score to settle with Benedick—his teasing soon comes very close to taunting. Benedick, he says, looks ridiculous, outfitted as he is not in one smart style but in a mixture of all the modish foreign styles of dress. Nevertheless, this attack on Benedick is more dangerous because it inadvertently allows Don Pedro to send Claudio a destructive message. Claudio himself is newly concerned with "carving the fashion of a new doublet," as Benedick said earlier (2.3.17–18)—he must be almost as absurdly dressed as his friend. By teasing Benedick and inviting Claudio to join him, Don Pedro in effect asks Claudio whether he wants to be a foolish young lover or the companion of an urbane and elegant prince.

The belief that young lovers are as foolish as their fashionable clothes represents Don Pedro's last line of defense, and Benedick now deprives him of his consoling thought. When Don Pedro and Claudio slyly argue over whether Benedick is in love, it is no accident that Don Pedro puts the negative case, asserting that there is "no true drop of blood" in Benedick (3.1.18–19). Benedick delivers a stunning refutation of Don Pedro's allegation. He proudly says to Leonato: "Walk aside with me, I have studied eight or nine wise words . . . which these hobby-horses must not hear" (ll. 71–73). That Benedick remains unperturbed testifies to the emotional strength the mere illusion of love gives the lover; Don Pedro registers shock: "For my life, to break with him about Beatrice." Suddenly, Don John enters as the tempter and says with grim irony, "My lord and brother, God save you!"

Like many great temptations in Renaissance literature, the success of this one depends on the predisposition of those tempted. Claudio, in his desire for a marriage that will bring him honor, has long been concerned to know that Hero is "modest." He has now been made to feel that for an uncertain future he may forego Don Pedro's assured patronage. The prince has gradually succumbed to his own fear of the isolation that will follow the loss of Claudio to marriage. Finally, the temptation has been prepared for by showing that Don Pedro takes pride in the support he has given Claudio and society in general; he will not consciously be false to his ideals, but he may be easily convinced that he should protect Claudio from a marriage that will disgrace him.

When Don John announces that he has news showing the marriage to be ill-advised, Don Pedro puts himself forward as Claudio's protector. Then, when Don John accuses Hero of being "disloyal" (3.2.104), the prince waits until Claudio inquires of him: "May this be so?" "I will not think it," Don Pedro replies. Even to the modern ear, his words imply that only his magnanimous mind stands against a sea of evidence. In Elizabethan English, the verb *think* distinguishes mental process from external reality, as in Hamlet's observation, "There is nothing either good or bad, but thinking makes it so" (2.2.249–50). Claudio catches Don Pedro's insinuation and quickly promises to watch at Hero's window. Then Don Pedro concludes, "O day untowardly turn'd!" and Claudio echoes him, "O mischief strangely thwarting!" (ll. 131–32). At this point, Claudio clearly contemplates shaming Hero in the church, and Don Pedro indicates a willingness to back him (ll. 125–27). Thus it is not surprising that later they both believe not only Don John's flimsy visual evidence, but the totally unsubstantiated charges about how Hero has already met her lover "a thousand times in secret" (4.1.94).

In the Bandello novella that is a probable source for *Much Ado,* Sir Timbreo (Claudio's equivalent), though hardly an admirable person at this point in the story, quietly repudiates Hero in a private communication sent to her father. By moving the scene into the church, Shakespeare not only creates effective theater; he puts Claudio and Don Pedro into a far worse light. Claudio allows Hero and her family to anticipate the marriage and then he suddenly insults her, in the harshest terms: "Give not this rotten orange to your friend," he tells the shocked father (4.1.32). Pouring forth a torrent of abuse, Claudio depicts himself as a pathetic and larmoyant victim of woman's "savage sensuality" (l. 61). If he can be seriously thought of as a rounded human character (as I think it likely), this catalogue of stereotypical abuse is an index of a lava of desires that as a proper young suitor he has been forced to repress; towards Hero he has shown only "bashful sincerity and comely love" such as "a brother to his sister" shows (ll. 53–54). "You are dishonorable, not me," he seems to insist in the church.

Don Pedro justifies his role by claiming that he acts reluctantly and only because his protégé has been wronged. Yet he, no less than Claudio, tries to inflict maximum pain. He waits until a critical moment, then instructs Claudio to "render [Hero] again" to her father. "Sweet Prince, you learn me noble thankfulness," is Claudio's deeply ironic response (l. 30). That Don Pedro has become the teacher confirms his failure to master the "hard lesson" Claudio once asked of him. Don Pedro also speaks with devastating effect when Leonato, innocently trustful, turns to him: "Sweet Prince, why speak not you?" Then Don Pedro does speak: "I stand dishonor'd, that have gone about / To link my dear friend to a common stale" (ll. 64–65). The audience knows the prince is wrong and perhaps even senses complacency.

As Hero faints, and is perhaps thought to be dying, the three parties leave, in a final gesture of contempt: Don John, followed by Don Pedro and Claudio. Those who remain at Hero's side—Leonato, Beatrice, Benedick, and the friar who was to have performed the wedding ceremony—now have their moral fiber tested. They are concerned for Hero's life, outraged at the treatment she has received, and doubt (at least) that the charges against her are true. The friar—a figure partially detached from the society—provides exemplary faith in Hero's innocence, having noticed her "thousand" innocent blushes when her crimes were named. Beatrice also behaves admirably. She cries out in alarm when Hero falls, gives her comfort when she begins to stir, and testifies to her innocence: "Oh, on my soul, my cousin is belied!" (l. 146).

Leonato, on the other hand, at once takes the accusations to be true: "Would the two princes lie, and Claudio lie?" he asks (l. 152), showing his limitations: he is a superficial man, unable to imagine that a contradiction might exist between exalted rank and inner worth. But while his credulity is forgivable, his vanity and self-absorption are more serious faults, since they lead him to heinous behavior. When Hero begins to stir, he tells her: "Do not live" (l. 123). Better she had been a changeling, he says, so that now, "smirched . . . and mired in infamy" as she is, he would not need to acknowledge her as his own daughter. Of course the harshness is intended to be an index of the severity of the charge and the importance of the code presumed violated. And yet as Leonato strings up what seems like a declension of first person personal and possessive pronouns, a note of self-centeredness is very clear in his lament: "Mine I lov'd, and mine I prais'd, / And mine that I was proud on, mine so much / That I myself was to myself not mine, / Valuing of her" (ll. 136–39). Leonato had "valued" his daughter as a flattering possession; the marriage he desired for her—to a count with royal connections—was to redound to the credit of his family, indeed, to *his* credit. Once Hero suffers "shame," he wants "no part" of her. Leonato's words are among the harshest any father in Shakespeare speaks to his child, and the harshest in all the comedies. Leonato is not an evil man, but his values are questionable.

Though Leonato and Hero respond to the crisis in almost opposite ways, both declare themselves unambiguously; on the other hand, Benedick's reaction puzzles. At first it seems that his remaining in the church reflects a moral decision to dissociate himself from his former friends and commit himself to the wronged family. But though Benedick is sympathetic, he continues to describe Don Pedro and Claudio as possessing his "inwardness and love" (l. 245), and he is noncommittal about the allegations against Hero: "I am so attir'd in wonder, / I know not what to say" (ll. 144–45). A satisfactory explanation for Benedick's presence has yet to emerge.

When Leonato, Hero, and the friar leave the church, Beatrice and Benedick remain. Shakespeare has cunningly planted a temptation for them. Having not been alone together since falling in love, they now have an opportunity to court, but under circumstances when their primary obligation should certainly be to Hero and not to themselves.

Benedick begins by comforting Beatrice, trying (for the first time) to sound convinced of Hero's innocence: "Surely I do believe your fair cousin is wrong'd" (ll. 259–60). Beatrice rightly sees that Benedick is making a tentative approach to her, and she wants to encourage him, at the same time that she contrives to prevent their "alliance" from conflicting with her loyalty to Hero. Beatrice shrewdly answers Benedick by remarking: "Ah, how much might the man deserve of me that would right" Hero (ll. 261–62). Then when Benedick volunteers to be that man, Beatrice tells him: "It is a man's office, but not yours." She goads Benedick to prove his valor, while also implying that he must choose whether he is committed to his friends or to her family. Benedick promptly takes Beatrice's hint and renounces one allegiance by declaring another: "I do love nothing in the world so well as you." They quickly drop mention of Hero and talk of love.

Eventually the conversation does return to Hero, but only because Benedick moves out of his depth. Though Beatrice has asked him to avenge her family, Benedick cannot conceive how disturbed Beatrice is both by the wrong done her cousin and her own present neglect of Hero's cause. Benedick's ignorance and his penchant for the grand gesture lead him to present himself as a knight errant ready to prove his worth to his ladylove: "Come, bid me do any thing for thee"

(l. 288). Though initially cautious when they spoke of love, Beatrice had gradually been swept along on a tide of enthusiasm; hearing these words, however, she remembers the Benedick of old, a man of many words but little faith. Instinctively, she challenges him to meet her highest expectations: "Kill Claudio." Taken completely by surprise, Benedick exclaims: "Ha, not for the wide world."

Beatrice now must make a choice. She can accept Benedick as he is, or repudiate him, or attempt to have him see with her eyes. She seems to end the interview, but her witty reply betrays her: "You kill me to deny it [i.e., the request]. Farewell." Benedick detains her, and she stays, but not without confronting him with the reasons for her anger:

> Is [Claudio] not approv'd in the height a villain, that hath slander'd, scorn'd, dishonor'd my kinswoman? O that I were a man! What, bear her in hand [deceive with false hopes] until they come to take hands, and then with public accusation, uncover'd slanders, unmitigated rancor—O God, that I were a man! . . . Princes and counties! Surely a princely testimony, a goodly count, Count Comfect, a sweet gallant surely! O that I were a man for his sake! or that I had any friend would be a man for my sake! But manhood is melted into cur'sies, valor into compliment, and men are only turn'd into tongue, and trim ones too. He is now as valiant as Hercules that only tells a lie, and swears it.
>
> (4.1.301–6, 315–22)

Of interest is the fact that Beatrice focuses her indictment of Claudio not on his decision to break the engagement, but on his way of disrupting the wedding ceremony. It would seem that she has detected beneath his mincing manner a sadistic urge that led him to calculate Hero's humiliation. Beatrice has measured the man; she realizes, as Leonato does not, that titles may mislead. Claudio is nothing more than a "sweet gallant," a spoiled young aristocrat. Beatrice widens her view to encompass Don Pedro and Don John—they have provided "princely testimony," she remarks bitterly—and then broadens her scope still further to take in all of "manhood" as she has observed it in her society. She sees that an ostentatious display of courtesy hides the absence of real courtesy; honor comes at a risk; better to guard one's social position and simply appear honorable.

Beatrice speaks with the authority she has gradually accumulated since the opening scene, in which she sought to discover the reality everyone else was busy to ignore. She interprets the repudiation of Hero as more than an isolated event; she sees it as confirming doubts she has long entertained—not necessarily specific doubts about specific people, but a general suspicion that extrinsic and intrinsic honor have become confused in her society. Though Beatrice's tirade is delivered in the heat of passion, it nevertheless contains, I believe, a core of truth.

The church scene tests and exposes a society in miniature. In Don Pedro, Claudio, and Leonato grievous flaws are uncovered, and in Beatrice and Benedick, potentially significant weaknesses. At the bitterest moments during the scene, one might complain with Berowne in *Love's Labour's Lost* that Jack hath not Jill and the play nothing resembles a comedy. Yet this scene has several hints that Jack *will* have Jill, and the following scene contains more. The friar, making an attempt to comfort Leonato, suggests a ruse: the family should pretend that Hero is dead; he hints at a miraculously happy outcome and goes so far as to say, "this wedding-day / Perhaps is but prolong'd" (ll. 253–54).

The interview between Beatrice and Benedick also gives strong indications that this match will go forward. Then in the second scene of act 4, Dogberry enters with the nightwatchmen and their prisoners, Borachio and Conrade. The audience already knows that the nightwatchmen overheard a drunken Borachio confess the details of Don John's plot to Conrade. Disclosure of the plot was delayed only because Leonato was in haste to join the wedding party and because he and Dogberry, equally self-important personages, spoke at cross-purposes. However, the sexton proves an efficient investigator. Already informed that Don John has fled the city, he quickly ascertains the nature of his crimes. It seems likely that at least a considerable portion of the blame will light on Don John; if it does, Don Pedro and Claudio may be reconciled to Leonato and the planned marriage may yet go forward. By the end of act 4, therefore, Shakespeare has not left great doubt about the externals of the plot.

Act 4 has, however, raised questions about the "inward changes" which will be the focus of the last act. The characters all have another test to confront. They have a chance to redeem themselves and prove worthy of the celebration that lies in the offing. Or they can merely resume the rush to the altar, once their knowledge of Don John's crime permits him to serve as their scapegoat.

Specific questions about individual characters have emerged during act 4. In suggesting his ruse to Leonato, the friar predicts that "slander" will change to "remorse" when the princes and Claudio receive news of Hero's death (l. 211). Of Claudio, in particular, the friar says that "if ever love had interest in his liver," and regardless of whether Claudio continues to believe Hero guilty, knowledge of her death will make him regret her loss and contemplate the beauties in her life (ll. 222–33). If the friar is right, Claudio will gain an appreciation for Hero that he has never had, and Don Pedro will recommit himself to true courtesy.

The friar also helps to establish the test facing Leonato. Shocked by Leonato's loss of faith in Hero, the friar urges on him belief in his daughter's innocence. Although Leonato at first rejects the suggestion, he eventually admits the possibility. He is still more concerned with his own dignity than with Hero's plight, however. When he promises revenge against the princes and Claudio if they are guilty, he seems eager to impress others that he is not a man to be trifled with (ll. 190–200). He lacks all conviction about who is at fault, and he eventually agrees to follow the friar's plan by saying: "Being that I flow in grief, / The smallest twine may lead me" (ll. 249–50). About all that can be said in favor of Leonato is that for the moment he accepts the advice of well-intentioned people: he remains susceptible to beneficent influences.

Beatrice and Benedick also have yet to prove themselves. That they will eventually marry there is little doubt. But will they, as a couple, exert moral authority? If others do not, will they at least call Don Pedro and Claudio to account? From their relationship thus far, an answer to this question probably depends on the answer to another: Will Benedick defer to Beatrice's greater wisdom, or will she gratify Benedick by accepting the subordinate role?

In the course of act 5, the anticipated justification for a celebration develops: major blame for the slander of Hero is attributed to Don John. Whether the audience accepts this interpretation of events depends in part upon the judgments it made in the earlier acts; if viewers were critical, they will find ample reason for remaining so. The sequence of the act itself invites suspicions. The first three scenes immediately follow the interrupted wedding; the last scene takes place the next morning. In other words, in a trice of time, the march to the altar resumes. Has an adequate investigation taken place, or has Messina chosen Don John as a scapegoat in order to remove an impediment to marriage?

Doubts about Leonato's character are kept alive by his conversation with his brother, Antonio, at the beginning of act 5. Leonato takes no comfort in Hero's survival; nor does he once regret the harsh words he spoke to her. His concern is still not his daughter's suffering, but his own, which, however, he expresses in hyperbolical language that cannot possibly represent true passion. No father has grieved as he grieves, and no father "so lov'd his child" (5.1.8)—a preposterous claim, one might think. In everything Leonato says, he implies a subtext: "I'm an important person who has been affronted." Leonato acts the lordly paterfamilias who feels sorrows inaccessible to his brother. When Don Pedro and Claudio enter, the two brothers foolishly compete to show greater concern for the insult the family has suffered. A. P. Rossiter describes them as "two old men lashing themselves back into a youthful fury." First Leonato, then Antonio, challenges Claudio, as if each is trying to outdo the other. The challenges bring to the fore a question about Leonato's motives. By maintaining the fiction of Hero's death, Leonato leaves open the friar's suggestion, that Don Pedro and Claudio will seek a rapprochement with him. For all Leonato's bluster, he does not break decisively with the men who slandered his daughter.

As soon as Leonato learns from the sexton of Don John's flight, he confronts Don Pedro and Claudio, ironically calling them "a pair of honorable men" (l. 266) who should include Hero's death among their "high and worthy deeds" (l. 269). Leonato seems stern, but he has a ruse in mind. Responding to the offers of Don Pedro and Claudio to do penance, Leonato turns to the latter and asks him to go to Hero's grave that evening, where he should hang an epitaph on her tomb and sing a dirge (ll. 284–85). Then, as if requesting further restitution, Leonato instructs the men to return to his home the next morning, at which time Claudio should marry his niece.

Leonato's easily accomplished penance may merely reflect the dramatist's desire for a quick and happy denouement. Shakespeare has added one detail, however, that raises a question about Leonato's motives. Leonato states very carefully that his "niece" is sole heir to both himself and his brother (l. 290). As Claudio is a man interested in inheritances, Leonato's purpose seems clear: he has long ago decided that Count Claudio, with his royal connections, would make a good son-in-law, and he now wishes to consummate the union between the young man and his daughter.

The behavior of Claudio and Don Pedro in act 5 makes it difficult to believe that they undergo the reformation Leonato fails to require. The friar had expected Don Pedro and Claudio to repent upon hearing of Hero's death; instead they enter to taunt the father and uncle of the woman presumed killed. Don Pedro needles Leonato by curtly walking by him with the comment: "We have some haste" (5.1.47). Claudio puts his hand on his sword, then denies he would give Leonato's "age such cause of fear" (l. 56). Claudio and Don Pedro have continued their downward spiral. Don Pedro had been a model of courtesy until the church scene, during which he struck out at society, at the hated institution of marriage. When Don Pedro finds that no punishment is forthcoming and that he even retains Claudio's companionship, his habitual control partially breaks down, and he exercises a kind of drunken freedom. Of course, as royalty, Don Pedro knows how to hint antagonism and suggest a course for Claudio to follow, while he himself avoids an open, irreconcilable break with Leonato. Claudio, for his part, is no longer the well-behaved young man who arrived in Messina. He throws off the constraints he accepted when he sought Leonato's favor and becomes the snob Beatrice thought she detected in the church.

It is not until Leonato and his brother leave that Don Pedro and Claudio have a chance to express their full contempt for their host. As soon as Benedick enters, they tell him that, "We had lik'd to have had our two noses snapp'd off with two old men without teeth" (ll. 115–16). This remark earns a rebuke from Benedick, who then delivers his challenge to Claudio. At this point, Claudio and Don Pedro join in uncontrollable jesting at Benedick's haughty manner. Even after Benedick discloses in a parting comment news of Don John's flight, Claudio and Don Pedro continue to laugh at Benedick's pretensions, though Don Pedro, at least, knows it is time for him to be serious (ll. 203–5). When Dogberry enters with his prisoners, Borachio and Conrade, the prince amuses Claudio by parodying the foolish constable's speech. Only Borachio's somber confession gives Don Pedro pause:

> DON PEDRO: Runs not this speech like iron through your
> blood?
> CLAUDIO: I have drunk poison whiles he utter'd it.
>
> (5.1.244–46)

These lines suggest that residual levity may remain in both men, for Don Pedro describes how the news affects him by using a figure of speech that Claudio, as if amused, develops in his reply. Don Pedro's remark shows him distancing himself from the crime in still another way, as Horace Furness noticed: "How gracefully and adroitly the Prince evades all responsibility by the use of this 'your' instead of *our!*" Don Pedro makes another deft move. Guilt is still too close to him if he leaves it with Claudio, since the two have been constant companions. Therefore the prince gets Borachio to confirm that Don John instigated the plot, then emphatically describes his brother as "compos'd and fram'd of treachery" (l. 249). Don Pedro anticipates the use others will make of his brother; yet the prince, as well as anyone, knows Don John's evil nature. Rather than making a new discovery, Don Pedro merely finds a way to extenuate his guilt.

When an apparently angry Leonato accuses Don Pedro and Claudio, they say they are contrite; they are undoubtedly shaken by the discovery of Hero's innocence, yet they do not fully confront the wrong they have done. After offering to do penance, Claudio adds, "yet sinn'd I not, / But in mistaking" and Don Pedro (content on this occasion to be Claudio's echo) adds, "By my soul, nor I" (5.1.274–75). Their wrongdoing hardly seems merely a matter of having trusted the treacherous Don John. Nor is it only their reluctance to accept guilt that is disturbing. Don Pedro appears to patronize Leonato: "To satisfy this good old man, / I would bend under any heavy weight / That he'll enjoin me to" (ll. 276–77). And although Claudio with tears embraces Leonato's offer of his niece in marriage, he does so immediately following mention of the double dowry; is he partly moved by the sudden opportunity to restore himself to good social standing?

The dirge scene resolves none of the doubts that have arisen about the "inner changes" the two men have experienced. Shakespeare might easily have created the impression of protracted mourning by beginning the scene *in medias res.* Instead, the scene opens with the arrival in the churchyard of the two men and several musicians and singers. Claudio reads the epitaph and asks the singers to render a "solemn hymn" (5.3.11). Claudio fulfills Leonato's directions, doing no less— and no more—than was asked of him. Alexander Leggatt notices that Claudio's grief is expressed only through "external forms," never in personal terms, but argues that "formal expressions of feeling have their own kind of value." The scene remains ambiguous, however, because the reality that lies behind Claudio's willingness to conform to social rituals is questionable. The few words that Don Pedro and Claudio exchange between themselves lack a convincing indication of sorrow.

Even in the final scene Don Pedro and Claudio seem curiously detached from the suffering they think they have caused. When the men arrive at Leonato's, Don Pedro smartly teases Benedick, recalling to him his boast that he would die a bachelor. Claudio, still taking his cues from Don Pedro, elaborates upon the joke (5.4.40–47). Claudio has been accused of "flippancy," and rightly, I think. Asked whether he is prepared to fulfill his promise to marry Antonio's daughter, he replies, "I'll hold my mind were she an Ethiope" (l. 38). Then, when the masked women approach, he turns from Benedick, saying, "Here comes other reck'nings. / Which is the lady I must seize upon?" (ll. 52–53). The remark is not very gracious, to say the least. Claudio acts as if he feels compelled to go through with the wedding, but regards the situation as disagreeably beneath his dignity.

Beatrice and Benedick display in act 5 the willingness to compromise moral principle anticipated in their church interview. Benedick has already challenged Claudio in a pompous manner that makes it hard to take at face value the moral earnestness he alleges. His lack of gravity is amply illustrated when he searches for Beatrice to report having made the challenge. He has been writing sonnets—poor stuff, he admits—while insisting that in other ways, he is a "deserving" lover (5.2.29–41). Beatrice enters to ask: "What hath pass'd between you and Claudio?" "Only foul words—and thereupon I will kiss thee." Benedick's answer shows him unwilling to be serious and eager to divert Beatrice. As in the church interview, Beatrice feigns a departure, then engages in love talk.

Only a chance comment from Benedick brings to the surface Beatrice's underlying reservations. When Benedick casually remarks upon the extension of their accustomed repartee into the period of their courtship by saying, "Thou and I are too wise to woo peaceably" (l. 72), Beatrice's reply introduces unexpected caution: "It appears not in this confession; there's not one wise man among twenty that will praise himself." Benedick will not be gainsaid, however; he answers that in the present day and age, a man with a free conscience should be "the trumpet of his own virtues" (ll. 85–86). Promptly taking his own advice, Benedick testifies that he himself is "praiseworthy." Beatrice answers never a word, for she has learned her uncle's lesson at last: "Niece, thou wilt never get thee a husband, if thou be so shrewd of thy tongue" (2.1.18–19).

A servant suddenly brings Beatrice and Benedick news:

It is prov'd my Lady Hero hath been falsely accus'd, the
Prince and Claudio mightily abus'd, and Don John is the
author of all, who is fled and gone.

(5.2.96–99)

Once, in an outraged voice, Beatrice had shown Benedick that, regardless of whether Don Pedro and Claudio thought Hero guilty, they
treated her abominably. Neither Beatrice nor Benedick wish to remember the resolve they made then. Their one desire is to rush off and
join Hero and Claudio in a double wedding.

By now properly investigating the crime that took place and by
accepting perfunctory repentances, the family is able to celebrate two
marriages, as it has long desired to do. Audience response to the
celebration is shaped by the decision arrived at about the real nature of
the crime. I have yet to consider the light shed on this event by one
possible accomplice, Margaret, Hero's "waiting gentlewoman."

Margaret and Borachio are apparently lovers (2.2.12–14). In suggesting a plot to Don John, Borachio confidently assumes Margaret's
willingness to disguise herself as Hero in order to decoy Claudio into
thinking his fiancée is unfaithful (2.2.41–50). Subsequent evidence suggests that Borachio may have judged Margaret correctly. The night
before the planned wedding, the nightwatch overhears Borachio describe the incident that just took place. He says that he called Margaret
Hero and that Margaret answered to that name from her chamber-
window and bid him "a thousand times good night" (3.3.147–48).
Later Margaret is said to have dressed in Hero's garments (5.1.238).
When Leonato finally gets the information gathered by the nightwatch,
he questions Borachio about Margaret. Borachio, however, testifies
that she "knew not what she did when she spoke to" him (5.1.301).
Still suspicious, Leonato interrogates Margaret; at the opening of 5.4,
in Margaret's presence, Leonato settles upon a somewhat different
account from the one Borachio offered—she acted not unwittingly, but
"against her will" (5.1.5). Leonato exonerates her and she is included
in the celebration.

The critics have been satisfied with Leonato's verdict. They dis-
miss the evidence against Margaret, arguing either that it is too trivial
to notice in performance or that it represents something other than
Shakespeare's final intention, the survival from a source for the play,
perhaps, or an earlier version of *Much Ado* itself. One wonders, however, whether the strength of the evidence is sometimes overlooked

because it raises a question about the adequacy of Leonato's entire investigation and thus about the conventionally happy close of the comedy.

Margaret has a motive for the crime: resentment against her social betters. Margaret shows her character most fully when she helps Hero dress for her wedding (3.4). Margaret treats Hero as a spoiled rich girl. As Hero fusses over her clothes and seeks the attention she feels is her right on this occasion, Margaret first makes her uncomfortable about the choice of a ruff, and then obliquely deprecates Hero's gown by comparing its simplicity with the duchess of Milan's more lavish garment (ll. 14–23). Finally, Margaret shows up the prim and proper Hero by making a coarse allusion to marital sex. Hero rebukes her:

> HERO: Fie upon thee, art not asham'd?
> MARGARET: Of what, lady? of speaking honorably? Is not
> marriage honorable in a beggar? Is not your lord
> honorable without marriage?
>
> (3.4.28–31)

This excerpt perhaps makes a difficult passage more difficult; yet the drift of Margaret's remark is clear. She alludes to Heb. 13.4 (a passage incorporated in the Anglican marriage service), where marriage is declared "honorable in all." Margaret implies a contrast between the equality enjoined on man in the Bible and the inequality introduced by social distinctions: Hero's lord is "honorable without marriage"—he is the honorable Count Claudio. In the social world in which Margaret and Hero live, honor is achieved not by making any marriage but by a "good" marriage. Later, in a bawdy exchange with Benedick, Margaret expresses the desire for a marriage that will not leave her "below stairs" (5.2.10). Margaret has no such marriage in prospect, and she resentfully watches Hero's nuptial approach.

Margaret behaves, in fact, as if she might indeed have participated in the plot the previous evening and now sought to justify in her own mind the damage about to ensue. Whether or not Margaret did indeed conspire with Don John and Borachio the play does not demonstrate. Instead, Shakespeare uses Margaret to help develop the dark background against which Messina moves toward marriage. Margaret makes it harder to think of Don John's evil as singular; he emerges more clearly as part of a social context that includes characters in the mainstream of society.

It is difficult to maintain a sharp distinction between "good" and "evil" characters in the play. Don Pedro's destructive urge does not originate in Don John. The bastard prince succeeds because he is, in part, the destructive side of Don Pedro and the side that comes to prevail. In like manner, it is also possible that even without both princes, Claudio might have denounced Hero as he did. By putting his question to Benedick about Hero's chastity in the negative, he reveals that doubt already has a place in his mind: "Is she not a modest young lady?" Finally, Leonato's tirade against his daughter results from emotions elicited, but surely not caused, by the particular set of circumstances brought about by Don John's plot.

The enemy is within the gates of Messina. Beneath a thin veneer of civility, Messina is an anxious and insecure world where the men "hold their honors in a wary distance" (*Othello* 2.3.56). Uneasy about their social position, anxious to advance their fortunes, the characters keep a watchful eye, and as soon as they perceive danger, push cordiality aside. A quarrel almost develops after the dance, then flares out at the wedding. If the characters felt strong affection for one another, once the heat of the moment passed they would begin to seek a reconciliation; instead, acrimonious exchanges and challenges open act 5. The characters quarrel until Don John's flight makes it possible to think of marriage again; then they hastily conclude peace. Yet the celebration cannot wholly obliterate the tensions that surfaced. Benedick and Claudio exchange verbal blows with their old gusto until Benedick remembers that he must leave Claudio "unbruis'd" because through marriage they are about to become "kinsmen" (5.4.111).

Don Pedro is of course not part of the "alliance" concluded at Leonato's home, and the limits of kindness in Messina can be measured by the treatment accorded him. He is a foreign prince who had once been extended every courtesy. When he does not marry and fails as a matchmaker, he is no longer necessary to the household, though he is too important and too closely tied to Claudio to exclude or even treat with outright rudeness. The text of the play nevertheless provides hints (which can be developed in performance) that he is made subtly uncomfortable. When Don Pedro and Claudio offer to make restitution, Leonato gives instructions only to Claudio, although he does invite both men back to his home. When the men return, Don Pedro interjects himself into the conversation two or three times, but is not otherwise noticed until the last lines of the play. By this time, Benedick, pleased that he is marrying (as he thinks) despite social pressures, usurp's Leonato's role as master of ceremonies, even countermands

Leonato's order that the wedding should precede the festivities; then he addresses Don Pedro, now neglected and silent:

> Prince, thou art sad, get thee a wife, get thee a wife.
> There is no staff more reverend than one tipp'd with horn.
>
> (5.4.121–23)

This is the taunt of an insecure man. Even as Benedick goes to the altar, he needs to reassure himself by making Don Pedro feel left out. Benedick exhibits the hostility that has been part of Messina throughout the play and that helps to explain—though it does not excuse—the destructive acts of Don Pedro and the conspirators who malign Hero.

Broken Nuptials in Shakespeare's Comedies: *Much Ado about Nothing*

Carol Thomas Neely

Poised at the center of the comedies, the play looks both backward and forward. Its tensions and its poise are achieved by the interactions of its two plots, its two couples. None of the other comedies includes two such sharply contrasted, subtly interrelated, and equally important couples. While, despite some uneasiness about the issues, critics are generally in agreement that the Claudio/Hero story is the main plot and the Beatrice/Benedick story the subplot, they also concur that the subplot couple is rhetorically richer, dramatically more interesting, and psychologically more complex than the mainplot couple. Discrepancies in the sources, the tone, and the nature of the two plots have generated charges of disunity that have been countered by claims that the two are unified by one or another theme: giddiness, moral complacency, the deceptiveness of appearances. Varied, hesitant, or inadequate attempts to categorize the play, focusing usually on one plot or the other, also suggest that the relationship between the two plots has not been fully understood and confirm and illuminate *Much Ado*'s affinities with both festive and problem comedies.

C. L. Barber implies at a number of points in *Shakespeare's Festive Comedy* that *Much Ado* is like a festive comedy with a holiday world in which Beatrice and Benedick experience festive release; but the absence of an extended discussions suggests that it does not fit easily into his category. Sherman Hawkins, likewise emphasizing Beatrice and

From *Broken Nuptials in Shakespeare's Plays.* © 1985 by Yale University. Yale University Press, 1985.

Benedick, includes the play with *Comedy of Errors, Taming of the Shrew,* and *Twelfth Night* as a closed-heart comedy based on "sexual antago- nism" in which men and women must overcome internal obstacles to love; but his description fails to account for the Hero/Claudio plot. Northrop Frye, when attending to Beatrice and Benedick, likewise identifies the play as a humor comedy (like *Love's Labor's Lost* and *Taming*) in which the witty couple and Claudio must discard the humors that are impediments to love. But elsewhere Frye, focusing on Hero's death and rebirth, groups the play with *All's Well* as an exten- sion of the ritualistic "green-world" comedies—*Two Gentlemen of Ve- rona, Midsummer Night's Dream, As You Like It, Merry Wives of Windsor.* Other critics who emphasize the Hero/Claudio plot have also noted *Much Ado*'s connections with later plays. R. G. Hunter, in *Shakespeare and the Comedy of Forgiveness,* by stressing Claudio's error, contrition, and our forgiveness of him, is led to place the play at the beginning of a line stretching through *All's Well* to *Cymbeline* and *The Tempest*; but this forgiveness is only peripheral in *Much Ado.* Leo Salingar, as we have seen, places *Much Ado* in his category of problem comedies along with *Merchant of Venice, All's Well* and *Measure for Measure;* although *Much Ado* manifestly includes broken nuptials, the distinguishing mark of the category, the other characteristic features—the complex of the judge and the nun, the trial scene, and the conflict between justice and mercy—are attenuated or altogether absent, and the Beatrice/Benedick story does not fit the pattern. A. P. Rossiter, focusing on the themes and tone of the play rather than its plots, explores most fully and persuasively *Much Ado* as an immediate precursor of the group that he designates "problem plays" or "tragi-comedies"—*Henry IV, Part II, Troilus and Cressida, All's Well, Hamlet, Measure for Measure,* and *Othello.* He finds *Much Ado* balanced neatly on a tonal frontier between comedy and tragicomedy just before the "point at which a sense of humour *fails*" and is replaced by "cynicism"—"where the attitudes I called 'hardness' (self-defensive) and 'farce' (offensive, debunking) combine to 'place' love, honour, truth, only to devalue them."

As these various explorations suggest, *Much Ado about Nothing* combines elements from almost all of the other comedies in a unique mixture. It is linked with both the romantic comedies and the problem comedies by virtue of the interactions of its two couples, its two plots. In the Claudio/Hero plot, the anxieties and risks underlying the con- ventions of romantic love are expressed and contained by the broken nuptials, Hero's vilification and mock death, and Claudio's penitence and acceptance of a substitute bride, motifs that are developed further in *All's Well, Measure for Measure,* and the late romances. In the Beatrice/ Benedick plot, the mutual mockery, double gulling, and Benedick's acceptance of Beatrice's command to "Kill Claudio" function, as do the mockery, trickery, parody, and tamings of the festive comedies, to break down resistance and to release desire and affection. The Beatrice/ Benedick plot protects the Hero/Claudio plot by ventilating and displacing it and by transforming its romance elements. In turn, the impasse of the Hero/Claudio plot generates movement in the Beatrice/ Benedick plot and, by permitting the witty couple the expression of romantic affection, initiates the transformation of their "merry wars" into a witty truce. Together the two plots release and control elements that will generate greater uneasiness and distrust in the problem comedies. Together they maintain an equilibrium between male control and female initiative, between male reform and female submission, which is characteristic of the romantic comedies but is disrupted in the problem comedies. In this play, wit clarifies the vulnerability of romantic idealization while romance alters the static, self-defensive gestures of wit.

The two plots are played out against a backdrop of patriarchal authority, which is protected by the extensive bawdy, especially the cuckoldry jokes, and contained by the ineffectuality of the men's exercise of power, especially when exaggerated in the Dogberry subplot. The play's lighthearted, witty bawdy expresses and mutes sexual anxieties; it turns them into a communal joke and provides comic release and relief in specific ways. It manifests sexuality as the central component of marriage and emphasizes male power and female weakness. Its clever, inventive innuendo emphasizes the anatomical "fit" between the sexes: "Give us our swords; we have bucklers of our own" (5.2.19).

The bawdy persistently views sex as a male assault on women. Men "board" (2.1.138) women, "put in the pikes" (5.2.20), and women cheerfully resign themselves to being "made heavier . . . by the weight of a man," and "stuff'd" (3.4.26, 62–63). The women counterattack by mocking the virility that threatens them: the "blunt foils" (5.2.14), "short horns" (2.1.22), and "fine little" wit (5.1.161) of the men. They do not, however, see their own sexuality as a weapon. They joke about female "lightness" (3.4.36, 43, 45) to warn each other against it, not to threaten men; even the term itself identifies women with weakness rather than strength.

But women's proverbial "lightness" is also a source of power. Women fear submission to men's aggressive sexual power. Men, likewise perceiving sexuality as power over women, fear its loss through female betrayal. They defend themselves against betrayal in three ways: they deny its possibility through idealization, anticipate it through misogyny, or transform it, through the motif of cuckoldry, into an emblem of male virility. As Coppélia Kahn shows, cuckoldry is associated with virility through the horn, which symbolizes both. The reiterated motif "In time the savage bull doth bear the yoke" (1.1.254) emphasizes the bull's potency as well as his submission to dull domestic life and inevitable cuckoldry. Similarly, to be "horn-mad" (1.1.262) is to be both furious with jealousy and sexually voracious; both halves of the pun imply aggressiveness. The defensive function of these jokes is especially apparent in the extended one that precedes the couples' pledge to marry. In it the scorn due the cuckold is ingeniously swallowed up in the acclaim awarded the cuckolder for his "noble feat" by which he attains power over both the woman and the husband:

> CLAUDIO: Tush, fear not, man! We'll tip thy horns with gold,
> And all Europa shall rejoice at thee,
> As once Europa did at lusty Jove
> When he would play the noble beast in love.
>
> (5.4.44–47)

All rejoice with the woman. The cuckold is crowned, the cuckolder is noble, and even the illegitimate calf will be proud of, if intimidated by, his father's virility—and may even inherit it.

> BENEDICK: Bull Jove, sir, had an amiable low.
> And some such strange bull leaped your father's cow
> And got a calf in that same noble feat
> Much like to you, for you have just his bleat.
>
> (5.4.48–51)

Here Benedick implies that Claudio, like his putative father, may become a cuckolder, and Claudio subsequently jokes that Benedick, too, may be a "double-dealer" (5.4.114). Cuckoldry has thus been deftly dissociated from female power and infidelity and identified instead with masculine virility and solidarity, which are emphatically reasserted on the eve of the weddings.

Marriage and cuckoldry, both potentially threatening to male bonds and power, have become assurances of them. But male authority in the play remains lame and diffused. Leonato is a weak father; Claudio, a passive protagonist; Don John, a conventional villain. Don Pedro is potentially the most powerful man in the play by virtue of his age, rank, and multiple connections with the others. But this potential remains subdued. He phases himself out of the plots he initiates, is moved from the center of the action to the periphery, and is curtailed as a rival suitor. His illusory competition with Claudio for Hero is abruptly dropped, and what could become a courtship of Beatrice—"Will you have me, lady," (2.1.314)—when politely dismissed by her as a joke, is immediately abandoned in favor of the project of uniting her with Benedick. The men's rivalry evaporates, and their violence is defused. First Leonato's and Antonio's attempts to avenge Hero are comically presented, and then Benedick's challenge is laughed off.

Male power in the play also remains benign because it is blunted by its ineffectuality and rendered comic by Dogberry's parody of it. Most of the men's schemes—Pedro's to woo Hero, the Friar's to reform Claudio, Don John's and Leonato's to get revenge, Benedick's to kill Claudio, the Watch's first to "offend no man" (3.3.80) and later to bring wrongdoers to justice—are botched, backfire, or fall apart. But though none of the schemes works as it is supposed to, they all achieve their goals. Dogberry's bungling attempts to arrest Borachio and Conrade on some charge or other mirror and parody the inept strategy and good luck of the other men. Whereas at the end of the church scene Beatrice and Benedick transcend melodrama and create witty romance, in the following scene (4.2) Dogberry transforms melodrama downward into farce, parodying the perversions inside the church. The arraignment precedes any examination of the evidence, malefactors and benefactors are confused with each other, and judges as well as accused have charges brought against them. When, at the end of the scene, Dogberry defends himself, he becomes a comic spokesman for his betters. He endearingly articulates the men's testy response to insults real or imagined, their reliance on conventions—of dress, rank, wit, institutions—to protect and confirm their self-importance, and the potential for asininity that goes along with their desires for swaggering and safety:

> I am a wise fellow; and which is more, an officer; and which is more, a householder; and which is more, as pretty a piece of flesh as any is in Messina, and one that knows the law, go to! And a rich fellow enough, go to! And a fellow that hath

had losses; and one that hath two gowns and everything
handsome about him.

(4.2.80–86)

The play's presentation of male power is further symbolized by
the sheerly linguistic invention, "the Prince's officer Coxcomb" (4.2.72),
whose denomination suggests deference and pride, elegant arrogance
and assinine folly, but also embodies comfortable security. Such security is threatened by those outsiders who wish to usurp legitimate
authority and who are perhaps symbolized by Coxcomb's antithesis,
the "thief Deformed": " 'a has been a vile thief this seven year; 'a goes
up and down like a gentleman" (3.3.125–27). Yet in spite of the men's
rivalry, ineffectuality, and silliness, all of the play's plot-generating
deceits and revelations are controlled by them, and it is they who fit
women with husbands. Their authority and solidarity are confirmed in
the play's conclusion, which reconciles male power and alliances with
marriage.

But first conflicts disrupt both the male bonds and the two couples. The Claudio/Hero alliance is thinly sketched as a conventional
one in which the functions of romantic idealization are made clear.
Claudio protects himself from Hero's sexuality by viewing her as a
remote, idealized love object who is not to be touched or even talked
to: "she is the sweetest lady that ever I looked on" (1.1.183). Patriarchal
marriage customs conveniently coalesce with romantic rhetoric, ena-
bling him to maintain Hero as an object of social exchange and possession: "Lady, as you are mine, I am yours," he cautiously vows (2.1.296).
He lets Don Pedro do his wooing for him. He scarcely acknowledges
Hero's sexual attractiveness, and his only reference to his own desires
seems oddly passive and gynocentric in a play crammed with aggres-
sively phallic innuendo: "But now I am returned and that war-thoughts /
Have left their places vacant, in their rooms / Came thronging soft
and delicate desires, / All prompting me how fair young Hero is"
(1.1.294–97). Claudio thus alleviates his anxieties about marriage by
viewing it both as a romantic ideal and as a conventional social arrangement that will occupy the time between battles. Once married,
he intends to go off to Aragon immediately with Don Pedro, their
companionship uninterrupted (3.2.3).

Hero's willingness to be the passive object of her father's negotia-
tions, Don Pedro's decorous wooing, and Claudio's low-keyed proposal provide her with a parallel defense against sexuality. She is as

unforthcoming as Claudio at their first exchange, and perhaps she welcomes his silence, for she asks Don Pedro as he begins his wooing to "say nothing" (2.1.83). Her own uneasiness about sex is suggested in her unhappiness on her wedding day, and the one bawdy innuendo that she contributes to the banter, "There, thou prickest her with a thistle" (3.4.74) is as tentative as Claudius's allusion. Hero is the perfect object of his "delicate" desires: modest, chaste, virtuous, silent.

The witty verbal skirmishes comprising Beatrice's and Benedick's "merry wars" explicitly express the anxieties about loss of power through sexuality, love, and marriage that lie beneath Claudio's and Hero's silent romanticism. Their verbal wars fill up the silence of the Hero/Claudio plot and reveal the fundamental asymmetry of the battle of the sexes. Benedick expressly equates loving with humiliation and loss of potency; he imagines it as a castrating torture: "Prove that ever I lose more blood with love than I will get again with drinking, pick out mine eyes with a ballad maker's pen and hang me up at the door of the brothel house for the sign of blind Cupid" (1.1.243–47). He likewise fears being separated from his friends by marriage and loss of status with them if he must "sigh away Sundays" or, feminized, "turn spit" like Hercules (1.1.196; 2.1.244). He defends himself against a fall into love and marriage and against fears of female betrayal by distrust of women—"I will do myself the right to trust none" (1.1.237). Distrust, coupled with the claim that all women dote on him, allows him to process virility without putting it to the proof. Mocking Claudio's romantic idealization, he is similarly protected by misogyny; the parallel function of the two poses is evident in Benedick's admission that, could he find the ideal woman, he would abandon the pose: "But still all graces be in one woman, one woman shall not come into my grace" (2.3.27–29). As he continues his description of the ideal woman, it is clear that she, like Claudio's Hero, meets the conventional prescriptions for a suitably accomplished and submissive wife: "Rich she shall be, that's certain; wise, or I'll none; virtuous, or I'll never cheapen her; fair, or I'll never look on her; mild, or come not near me; noble, or not I for an angel; of good discourse, an excellent musician" (2.3.29–33). Benedick's misogyny puts him in a position of unchallengeable power; his wit is consistently belligerent, protective, and self-aggrandizing. But his bawdy incorporates, as romantic rhetoric does not, the aggressiveness and urgency of desire even while defending against it.

Instead of defensively asserting power and certainty, Beatrice's sallies often directly reveal weakness and ambivalence; her wit, in contrast to Benedick's, is consistently self-deprecating. Her mockery of marriage and men poignantly reveals her desire for both. The fear of and desire for women's roles that generate her merry mask are suggested in her description of her birth and her mother's response to it—"No, sure, my lord, my mother cried; but then there was a star danced, and under that was I born" (2.1.322–23)—and in Leonato's similarly paradoxical description of her—"She hath often dreamt of unhappiness and waked herself with laughing" (2.1.333). Her repartee, like that of the others, embodies anxiety about being unmarried, as it does about being married: "So, by being too curst, God will send you no horns" (2.1.23). She does not mock Hero's marriage plans as Benedick does Claudio's but only urges her to marry a man who pleases her. Hero's engagement does not engender smug self-satisfaction in her but a sense of isolation: "Thus goes everyone in the world but I, and I am sunburnt. I may sit in a corner and cry 'Heigh-ho for a husband!' " (2.1.306–8). Even her allusion to "living as merry as the day is long" in heaven "where the bachelors sit" shows her desire to continue to share equally in easy male camaraderie rather than a desire to remain single (2.1.45–47).

Beatrice's ambivalence about marriage is rooted in her fear of the social and sexual power it grants to men. Her bawdy jests manifest both her desire for Benedick and her fear of the potential control over her which her desire gives him. In the first scene it is she who quickly shifts the play's focus from Claudio's deeds of war to Benedick's deeds of love. She refers to him as "Signior Mountanto," suggestively initiates dialogue by asking, "Is it possible Disdain should die while she hath such food to feed it as Senior Benedick?" (1.1.29, 117), and from behind the safety of her mask admits to Benedick (of him)—"I would he had boarded me" (2.1.137). But her jesting about the unsuitability of husbands with beards and those without them both mocks Benedick's beard and reveals her ambivalent attitude toward virility: "He that hath a beard is more than a youth, and he that hath no beard is less than a man; and he that is more than a youth is not for me, and that is less than a man, I am not for him" (2.1.34–37). Because she is apprehensive about the social and sexual submission demanded of women in marriage and wary of men's volatile mixture of earthly frailty with arrogant authority, Beatrice does not want a husband:

> Till God make men of some other metal than earth. Would
> it not grieve a woman to be overmastered with a piece of

valiant dust? To make an account of her life to a clod of
wayward marl? No, uncle, I'll none. Adam's sons are my
brethren, and truly I hold it a sin to match in my kindred.

(2.1.56–61)

Neither hating nor idealizing men, she does not wish to exchange
kinship with them for submission to them. Given the play's dominant
metaphor of sex as a male assault, the subordination demanded of
Renaissance women in marriage, and the valiant cloddishness of many
of the men in the comedies, Beatrice's fear of being "overmastered"
seems judicious. But her anxieties, like Benedick's, grow out of pride
and fear of risk as well as out of justified wariness.

Beatrice and Benedick, both mockers of love, cannot dispel these
anxieties or admit to love without intervention. The asymmetrical
gullings perpetrated by their friends (the "only love-gods" in this play,
2.1.372) resemble the ceremonies mocking men and the attacks on
female recalcitrance already examined. These garrulous deceits follow
upon and displace Hero and Claudio's silent engagement and confront
anxieties there left unspoken. As male and female anxieties are different, the two deceits are contrasting. The men gently mock Benedick's
witty misogyny while nurturing his ego. Their gentle ribbing of
Benedick's "contemptible spirit" is tempered with much praise of his
virtues; he is proper, wise, witty, and valiant "As Hector" (2.3.180–87).
They alleviate his fears about Beatrice's aggressiveness by a lengthy,
exaggerated tale of her desperate passion for him: "Then down upon
her knees she falls, weeps, sobs, bears her heart, tears her hair, prays,
curses—'O sweet Benedick! God give me patience!' " (2.3.148–50). The
story dovetails perfectly with his fantasy that all women dote on him
(and presumably it gratifies the other men to picture the disdainful
Beatrice in this helpless state). The men also reassure Benedick that
Beatrice is sweet and "out of all suspicion, she is virtuous" (ll. 160–61).
The gulling permits Benedick to love with his friends' approval while
remaining complacently self-satisfied. Even these protective assurances
of his power win from him only a grudgingly impersonal acknowledgment of his feelings: "Love me? Why, it must be requited" (2.2.219).
This he must justify by relying, like Claudio, on friends' confirmations
of the lady's virtue and marriageability, and by viewing marriage not
personally but conventionally as a social institution designed to control
desire and ensure procreation: "the world must be peopled" (l. 236).

The women's gulling of Beatrice is utterly different in strategy and effect. They make only one unembroidered mention of Benedick's love for her, and even that is interrogative—"But are you sure / That Benedick loves Beatrice so entirely?" (3.1.36–37). They praise *his* virtues, not Beatrice's. Instead of treating sex with detachment, as the men do with their joke about " 'Benedick' and 'Beatrice' between the sheet" (2.3.139), the women include an explicit, enthusiastic reference to it: "Doth not the gentleman / Deserve as full as fortunate a bed / As ever Beatrice shall couch upon?" (3.1.44–46). Throughout most of the staged scene, they attack at length and with gusto Beatrice's proud wit, deflating rather than bolstering her self-esteem. The men emphasize Beatrice's love whereas the women emphasize her inability to love as a means of exorcising it: "She cannot love, / Nor take no shape nor project of affection, / She is so self-endeared" (ll. 54–56). Beatrice, accepting unabashedly the accuracy of these charges—"Contempt, farewell! And maiden pride, adieu!" (l. 109)—is released into an undefensive and personal declaration of love and of passionate submission to Benedick: "Benedick, love on; I will requite thee, / Taming my wild heart to thy loving hand. / If thou dost love, my kindness shall incite thee / To bind our loves up in a holy band" (ll. 111–14). She views marriage not as a social inevitability but as a ritual expressing affectionate commitment. Benedick's "love" will be requited with "kindness," not merely with the production of "kind." And, unlike Benedick, she trusts her own sense of his worth more than her friends' praise: "For others say thou dost deserve, and I / Believe it better than reportingly" (ll. 115–16).

The effect of the gullings is to engender parallels between the two women and the two men and to emphasize differences between the men and women, manifesting in this way the connections between the two plots. Hero asserts herself for the first time during the gulling of Beatrice. She zestfully takes the lead in the mockery, parodying Beatrice's contemptuous wit and scorning her scorn; her vehemence perhaps reveals some resentment of Beatrice's domination and shows her own similar capacity for aggressiveness, realism, and wit. In their next scene together on her wedding day, Hero for the first time expresses her own apprehensiveness about marriage by being heavy of heart and refusing to join in the sexual banter of the other women. Like Hero, Beatrice is now "sick" with love, and her wit is out of tune. Claudio welcomes Benedick's lovesickness even more gleefully than Hero does Beatrice's. During the gulling, his comic descriptions of the doting Beatrice and the valiant Benedick are caricatures of his own romantic ideals, while his description of Beatrice dying for Benedick (3.3.173–77) hints at the violence, anxiety, and desire for female submission that lie beneath the romantic veneer. Benedick in love is, like Claudio, "sadder"; his wit is curtailed ("governed by stops"), and he has shaved off his beard, marking his new vulnerability (3.2.15, 56). Claudio, with the other men, takes advantage of him, reiterating his tale of Beatrice's "dying."

The anxieties about sexuality and submission that are the source of the men's lovesickness then erupt violently in Don John's slander. It is ironically appropriate that, though Hero has never talked to Claudio at all and he had "never tempted her with word too large" (4.1.52), he should immediately accept Don John's report that she "talk[ed] with a man out at a window" (4.1.308) as proof of her infidelity. Though he does not "see her chamber window ent'red" (3.2.108), this imagined act transforms defensive idealization to vicious degradation, as will occur later with Angelo, Troilus, Hamlet, Othello, Posthumus, and Leontes. His former cautious, silent worship inverted, Claudio denounces Hero at their wedding with extravagantly lascivious, but still conventional, rhetoric:

> Out on thee, seeming! I will write against it,
> You seem to me as Dian in her orb,
> As chaste as is the bud ere it be blown;
> But you are more intemperate in your blood
> Than Venus, or those pamp'red animals
> That rage in savage sensuality.
>
> (4.1.55–60)

He perverts the ceremony that had seemed to protect him and seeks from friends confirmation of her corruption, as he had formerly needed proof of her virtues.

When unanchored idealization turns to degradation here, nuptials are shattered more violently and irretrievably than in the other comedies. The possibility of future reconciliation is kept alive, however, by the Friar's scheme for Hero's mock death, by Dogberry and crew's knowledge of the truth about Don John's deceit, and by Beatrice's command to Benedick. The slander of Hero tempers Beatrice's commitment to love. But Claudio's failure of romantic faith in Hero parallels and helps to rectify Benedick's lack of romantic commitment to Beatrice. Both men, along with Hero, must risk a comic death and effect a comic transformation to affirm their love. Although only

Dogberry's revelation influences the plot, the three "deaths" function together to engender the play's comic reconciliations and festive release.

Hero's mock death, transforming the strategies of self-concealment through masking, disguise, or withdrawal practiced by women in romantic comedies, anticipates the development of the motif in later plays. The women in *Love's Labor's Lost* mask themselves, and they go into seclusion at the end; Kate plays shrew and Titania evades Oberon; Julia, Rosalind, Portia, and Viola are disguised. The literal masks of Beatrice and Hero at the ball mirror their defensive facades of wit and silence. But, unlike these festive disguises, women's mock deaths do not merely parody or postpone nuptials voluntarily; they are designed by the woman and/or her confidantes to mend nuptials shattered by the men. It is now not idealization of women which must be qualified but their slander and degradation which must be reformed. The mock death is both an involuntary, passive escape from degradation and a voluntary constructive means to alter it.

Hero's play death incorporates many of the elements found in later versions of the motif; the friar, who engineers the death with Leonato's approval, outlines its constructive purpose and potential effects. The death—real or imagined—of the slandered woman satisfies the lover's desire for revenge while alleviating his fear of infidelity: "Yet she must die, else she'll betray more men" (*Othello* 5.2.6). Then relief and guilt working together will change "slander to remorse" (4.1.210). Freed from the pain of desiring her and the fear of losing her, the lover can reidealize the woman, a process that is described in detail by the friar, walked through in this play, and dramatized more completely in *All's Well That Ends Well, Hamlet, Othello, Antony and Cleopatra, Cymbeline,* and *The Winter's Tale.*

> For it so falls out
> That what we have we prize not to the worth
> Whiles we enjoy it; but being lacked and lost,
> Why then we rack the value, then we find
> The virtue that possession would not show us
> Whiles it was ours. So will it fare with Claudio.
> When he shall hear she died upon his words,
> Th' idea of her life shall sweetly creep
> Into his study of imagination
> And every lovely organ of her life
> Shall come appareled in more precious habit,

> More moving, delicate, and full of life,
> Into the eye and prospect of his soul
> Than when she lived indeed.
>
> (4.1.216–29)

Through the death—pretended or actual—of the corrupted beloved, the lover can repossess her, purified. In this way, the friar hopes, the "travail" of restoring the image of the woman will culminate in a "greater birth" (4.1.212), her death in life.

But for women the strategy is bold, painful, and risky. Whereas in earlier comedies, female disguise, control, and wit brought men to their senses, in later ones, more disturbingly female submission generates male affection. Hero must put herself in the hands of the friar, practice patience, and accept, if the tricks fails, chaste seclusion in a religious retreat—the fate Hermia is threatened with in *Midsummer Night's Dream*, Helen pretends to in *All's Well That Ends Well*, and Isabella desires in *Measure for Measure*. Women pretend to die of unrequited love as Beatrice is said to be doing; they "die" sexually, validating male virility as Helen and Mariana do in bedtricks whose deceit makes them a form of mock death; and they die, or pretend to, as retribution for their imagined betrayals; Juliet undergoes a double confrontation with death—her deathlike swoon induced by the Friar's potion and her interment with dead bodies in the Capulet monument—before she actually dies; Hermione must remain in seclusion sixteen years. In the tragedies women actually die. But the woman's pretended or real death, even when combined with the vigorous defense of her virtues by her friends—Beatrice, the Countess, Emilia, Paulina—does not by itself ensure penitence. Ophelia's and Desdemona's deaths do engender in Hamlet and Othello the penitent reidealization the friar describes. But Juliet's and Cleopatra's mock deaths kill Romeo and Antony. Claudio's and Bertram's penitence is perfunctory and coerced. Claudio seems utterly unaffected by the death until Borachio testifies to Hero's innocence (as Emilia will testify to Desdemona's and the oracle to Hermione's); then reidealization is instantaneous: "Sweet Hero, now the image doth appear / In the rare semblance that I loved it first" (5.1.250–51). Only Antony and Posthumus forgive the woman without proof of her innocence. Only in *Antony and Cleopatra* and *Cymbeline* does the mock death by itself lead to the guilt, penitence, and forgiveness predicted by the friar. And only at last in *The Winter's Tale* does the death lead to penitence, transformation, and full reconciliation. Although the motif appears in all genres, playing dead can perhaps be seen as a female version of the tragic hero's literal and symbolic journeys. Its effect is not to transform the woman as the tragic hero is transformed, but to achieve the transformation of her image in the eyes of the hero and to alter and complicate the audience's view of her. The motif satisfies the male characters' fantasies of control and the audience's need to sympathize with the slandered women.

But in *Much Ado* the festive conclusion is not only made possible by Hero's mock death, Claudio's enforced penance, and Dogberry's apprehension of the "benefactors" who expose the deceit. Equally important is Benedick's willingness to comply with Beatrice's command to "Kill Claudio" (4.1.288). Benedick's acquiescence signals his transformation and reconciles him with Beatrice. Although the gullings bring Beatrice and Benedick to acknowledge their affections to themselves, they have not risked doing so to each other. The broken nuptials provide the impetus for this commitment. The seriousness of the occasion tempers their wit and strips away their defenses. Weeping for Hero, Beatrice expresses indirectly her vulnerability to Benedick, just as Benedick's assertion of trust in Hero expresses indirectly his love for Beatrice and leads to his direct, ungrudging expression of it: "I do love nothing in the world so well as you" (4.1.267). This reciprocates Beatrice's earlier vow to "tame her wild heart" for him. But the broken nuptials have encouraged Beatrice to be wary still; her vow is witty, and she asks for more than vows from Benedick, taking seriously his romantic promise, "Come, bid me do anything for thee." "Kill Claudio," she replies (4.1.287–88).

Extravagant and coercive as her demand may be, Benedick's willingness to comply is a necessary antidote to the play's pervasive misogyny and a necessary rehabilitation of romance from Claudio's corruption of it. Benedick's challenge to Claudio, by affirming his faith in both Hero's and Beatrice's fidelity, repudiates his former mistrust of women and breaks his bonds with the male friends who shared this attitude. Because romantic vows and postures have proved empty or unreliable—"But manhood is melted into cursies, valor into compliment, and men are only turned into tongue, and trim ones too" (4.1.317–20)—they must now be validated through deeds. The deed Beatrice calls for is of a special sort. Male aggression is to be used not in war but for love, not against women but on their behalf. Beatrice calls on Benedick to become a hero of romance in order to qualify his wit and verify his commitment to her. Similar transformations are

demanded by the women of other men in the comedies: the lords in
Love's Labor's Lost must test their wit and prove their vows during a
year of penance; Bassanio must relegate friendship to surety for his
marriage; Orsino and Orlando are led to abandon silly poses for
serious marriage vows. But while the grave estrangement of Claudio
and Hero is displaced by Beatrice's and Benedick's movement into
romantic love, the wits' love for each other is also protected by their
commitment to the cause of Hero. Beatrice can weep for her friend as
she does not weep for Benedick, and Benedick is "engaged" simultaneously to Beatrice and on behalf of Hero.

The scene of the challenge itself also deftly intertwines two tones—
the romantic and the comic—and the two plots. Although it shows the
bankruptcy of Claudio's wit, it also absorbs Benedick's challenge back
into a witty comic context before actual violence can disrupt this
context irrevocably. Benedick, having abandoned his wit, proposes to
substitute a sword for it: "It [wit] is in my scabbard. Shall I draw it?"
(5.1.126). Seriously challenging Claudio, he refuses to join in his
friend's effort to use wit to transform swords back into jests, a duel to
a feast, his adversary to a dinner: "he hath bid me to a calf's head and a
capon; the which if I do not carve most curiously, say my knife's
naught. Shall I not find a woodcock too?" (5.1.154–57). In fact, sword-
play *is* absorbed back into wordplay when the slandering of Hero is
revealed, Claudio guiltily does penance, and the challenge is dropped.
Benedick's delivery of it releases him and Beatrice into the affectionate
banter through which, "too wise to woo peaceably" (5.2.71), they
reanimate the conventions of romantic rhetoric as they did those of
romantic valor: "I will live in thy heart, die in thy lap, and be buried in
thy eyes; and, moreover, I will go with thee to thy uncle's" (5.2.99–101).
The dynamics of the Beatrice/Benedick plot invert and counteract
the dynamics of the Claudio/Hero plot. Whereas Hero must "die" in
response to Claudio's misogynistic fantasies of her corruption in order
to restore his romantic attachment, Benedick must agree to kill Claudio
in compliance with Beatrice's demand in order to establish the replace-
ment of witty misogyny by romantic affection.

At the conclusion, Claudio's and Hero's pat reaffirmation of their
wedding vows ignores rather than transforming the conflicts which
erupted through the broken nuptials. First Claudio performs a ritualistic but impersonal penance: "Pardon, goddess of the night, / Those that
slew thy virgin knight; / For the which, with songs of woe, / Round
about her tomb they go" (5.3.12–15). Then he asserts his faith in

women by agreeing to accept a substitute bride. But his willingness to "seize upon" any bride seems to suggest that the possessiveness and conventionality which fuel romance are not exorcised. When she unmasks, Claudio declares, "Another Hero," and it is Don Pedro who must assert the continuity between the two Heros, one "defiled" and destroyed, the other pure, a "maid": "The former Hero! Hero that is dead!" (5.4.62–65). But there is no sense of rebirth. Claudio and Hero give no sign of establishing a new relationship or of incorporating desire. They move mechanically back into their former roles: "And when I lived I was your other wife / And when you loved you were my other husband" (5.4.61). In the problem comedies, Bertram's and Angelo's repentance and acceptance of substitute brides is even less spontaneous; in them the crucial presence of two women at the endings— the one the chaste object of lust (Diana, Isabella), the other the substitute bride and enforced marriage partner (Helen, Mariana)—emphasizes the continuing division between idealization and degradation, between romance and desire, which is glossed over here.

In *Much Ado,* however, Beatrice and Benedick, displacing the Claudio/Hero plot one final time, create the festive conclusion. Disruptive elements continue to be expressed and exorcised in their bantering movement into marriage. Their refusal to love "more than reason" or other than "for pity" or "in friendly recompense" (5.4.74–93) acknowledges wittily the fear each still has of submission and the desire each has that the other be subordinate. They are finally brought to their nuptials only by a wonderfully comic "miracle," (l. 91) but one not dependent on removal of disguise, recognition of other kinds, or the descent of a god. The discovery of their "halting" sonnets signals their mutual release into the extravagance of romance and is followed by the kiss which, manifesting their mutual desire, serves as a truce in their merry wars. This kiss "stop[s]" Beatrice's mouth as she had earlier urged Hero to "stop" Claudio's at their engagement (5.4.97; 2.1.299). But while affirming mutuality in one way, the kiss ends it in another, for it silences Beatrice for the rest of the play. Similarly, other strong, articulate women are subdued at the ends of their comedies—Julia, Kate, Titania, Rosalind, Viola. This kiss, then, may be seen as marking the beginning of the inequality that Beatrice feared in marriage and that is also implicit in the framing of the wedding festivities with male jokes about cuckoldry, in the reestablishment of male authority by means of these jokes, and in Benedick's control of the nuptials.

This inequality is confirmed as Benedick presides over the play's conclusion, using his wit to affirm the compatibility of manhood, friendship, and marriage. Through the cuckoldry motif, Benedick has transformed a potentially humiliating submission in marriage into a proof of power. He likewise transforms the women's "light heels" into a sign of joy, not infidelity (5.4.119). His final unifying gesture invites Don Pedro to join him and Claudio in marriage to alleviate his sadness, attain authority, and reestablish ties with his war companions: "get thee a wife, get thee a wife! There is no staff more reverend than one tipped with horn" (5.4.122–25). Beatrice's and Benedick's sparring is transformed by the broken nuptials into romantic attachment, and Hero's mock death and the revelation of her innocence transform Claudio's degradation of her into a ritualistic penance. Throughout the comedies broken nuptials, even when initiated by men, give women the power to resist, control, or alter the movement of courtship. But with the celebration of completed nuptials at the end of the comedies, male control is reestablished, and women take their subordinate places in the dance.

While rejoicing in the festive conclusion of *Much Ado* we should perhaps remember Beatrice's acute satire on wooing and wedding— and their aftermath:

> Wooing, wedding, and repenting is as a Scotch jig, a measure, and cinquepace. The first suit is hot and hasty like a Scotch jig (and full as fantastical); the wedding, mannerly modest, as a measure, full of state and ancientry; and then comes Repentance and with his bad legs falls into the cinquepace faster and faster till he sink into his grave.
>
> (2.1.69–75)

Beatrice's description, which sees marriage as a precarious beginning, not a happy ending, is anticipated by the many irregular nuptials of earlier comedies and is embodied in the troubling open endings of *All's Well That Ends Well* and *Measure for Measure*. In these plays the balance between wit and romance, between male authority and female power is lost. The culmination "fantastical" romance and "hot and hasty" desire in a "mannerly modest" ceremony does not preclude the repenting which follows in the problem comedies and tragedies. In the romantic comedies "the catastrophe is a nuptial," as Armado proclaims with relish in his love letter to Jaquenetta (*Love's Labor Lost*, 4.1.78), but later nuptials prove to be catastrophic in a sense other than the one Armado consciously intends. His own reversal of customary nuptials by getting Jaquenetta pregnant before the ceremony foreshadows a source of difficulty. And in *Much Ado about Nothing* there is one final nuptial irregularity: the dancing begins even before the weddings are celebrated.

Mistaking in *Much Ado*

Karen Newman

Many readers of *Much Ado about Nothing* have remarked that its tragi-comic pattern sets it apart from Shakespeare's other romantic plays and links it with the so-called problem comedies. I want to turn finally to *Much Ado* because it brings us full circle to *Measure for Measure*. Unlike the threatened tragedy of *Measure for Measure,* however, the tragedy of *Much Ado* is apparent rather than real. Things appear to happen; all the characters at one moment or another are seduced into believing in appearances, and its two plots are linked by this common theme of credulity and self-deception. Readers of both plays have been troubled by the uneasy union of vehement and lifelike passions with the conventions of comedy, in *Much Ado* in 4.1, and in *Measure for Measure* in the shift from the first three acts to the last two. Of *Much Ado,* J. R. Mulryne complains that "the unlovable Claudio is too vividly and realistically portrayed (in the manner of a figure in tragedy)." Tillyard argues of *Measure for Measure* that the change to the conventions of comedy from the "more lifelike passions is too violent" and that the bed trick is not "a case of modern prudery unaware of Elizabethan preconceptions but an artistic breach of harmony." Shakespeare's persistent use of substitution, disguise and the language of mistaken identity in both plays establishes from the outset comic expectations in the audience which are ultimately fulfilled, but as Jean Howard has recently argued of *Measure for Measure,* the play

---

From *Shakespeare's Rhetoric of Comic Character: Dramatic Convention in Classical and Renaissance Comedy.* © 1985 by Karen Newman. Methuen, 1985.

Strains and distorts a comic paradigm Shakespeare had used many times before, and in so doing calls attention to the way in which any set of conventions, generic or otherwise, can betray its basic function of mediating between audience and author to create lifelike illusions and becomes instead a sterile mechanism inadequate to its task.

She goes on to claim that *Measure for Measure* is an experiment in which Shakespeare attempts to escape from conventional comic formulas without losing his audience's "power to comprehend." Though I find this view persuasive, I would like to qualify it by suggesting that the "problem" of *Measure,* and that of *Much Ado* as well, is not so much the inadequacies of art and its conventions "to create a satisfactory illusion of lifelike complexity," but the uneasy union of the traditional comic plot designed to call attention to artifice, coincidence and wonder, with the conventions of realistic characterization, particularly the rhetoric of consciousness. In *Much Ado,* 4.1, and in *Measure for Measure,* Shakespeare uses such conventions so forcefully that our willingness to accept the artifice of their comic plots is undermined. Instead of extending the metaphorical power of mistaken identity by shifting its emphasis from plot to character, from external to psychological or internal mistaken identity, Shakespeare undermines our comic expectations by exaggerating the conventions of lifelike characterization in these plays. In *Much Ado,* Claudio is presented as a type common to Shakespeare's comedy, the courtly lover, but in 4.1, Shakespeare endows him with an inner life which conflicts with the type. So also in *Measure for Measure* the conventions of realistic characterization Shakespeare uses in portraying Angelo and Isabella conflict with the duke's intrigue plot. The "problem" of the two plays is not real passions versus comic conventions, as is so often claimed, but two kinds of opposing conventions, one which calls attention to itself and its artifice, the other which conceals itself by seeming "real."

There are, of course, obvious differences between the two plays which make the labels romantic comedy and problem play appropriate. *Much Ado* does, after all, have the strictly comic plot of Beatrice and Benedick, which embraces rather than disapproves of sexuality; it has Dogberry and the watch strategically placed to assure us that all will be well instead of the problematic Duke whom Lucio slanders and whose improvisations with Ragozine's head seem uncomfortably forced. And *Much Ado* ends with the marriage of its lovers, not with a judgment scene in which the Duke calls for and administers an Old Testament vengeance to Lucio and proposes marriage to the silent Isabella. But we need to look first at Shakespeare's portrayal of Claudio before we can compare *Much Ado* and *Measure for Measure* and assess their similarities and differences.

In *Much Ado*, Claudio mistakes Hero's true nature, discovers his error, and believing it has caused Hero's death, must atone for his "sin." Mistaken identity provides the means whereby both the mistake and Claudio's subsequent development is communicated to the audience. Like so many comic heroes, Claudio must lose in order to find. This fundamental pattern, which we have seen elsewhere, is juxtaposed with Beatrice and Benedick's parallel discovery of their mutual love.

Claudio's character, like Angelo's, has always seemed to trouble readers of *Much Ado*. Cynics claim he woos Hero for her money; romantics counter that his query about Leonato's family stems from timidity and embarrassment. It is perhaps anachronistic to fault Claudio because he asks about Hero's financial expectations, for even the cynical Benedick believes his friend's devotion is real. But our discomfort with Claudio's repudiation of Hero in the church scene is less easily dismissed. Before we consider 4.1, however, we need to look at how Shakespeare introduces Claudio and establishes the romance plot.

The play's first lines present Claudio as the courtly ideal: "he hath borne himself beyond the promise of his age, doing, in the figure of a lamb, the feats of a lion: he hath indeed better bettered expectation" (1.1.12–15). His falling in love with Hero is equally conventional. Before she utters a word, he loves her, and though not at first sight, from the moment of seeing her after his return from the wars. His language is that of the courtly lover: "In mine eye, she is the sweetest lady that ever I looked on" (ll. 174–75). He asks "Can the world buy such a jewel?" (l. 168), and as his verb suggests, he betrays a mercantile attitude toward love. Claudio needs assurance that others value his "jewel of price" and seeks confirmation of his love from Benedick.

Don Pedro's offer to woo Hero for Claudio triggers the first "suppose" of the play. A servant overhears this conversation, reports it to Leonato, who then believes Pedro woos Hero for himself. Claudio in turn believes Don John's tale of Pedro's love for Hero so that the action of the masked ball, as many have noted, prepares for the villain's intrigue by demonstrating Claudio's credulity and lack of self-confidence. His excessive idealism, untempered by compassion or

Wedding

by the sense of play which characterizes Beatrice and Benedick, ex-
plains how he can be duped by Don John's disguise plot. Though he
participates in the game of gulling the two would-be lovers, he hasn't
the imagination to include play in his own lovemaking.

John Anson argues that the balcony scene is a fantasy enactment of
Claudio's own fears and subconscious desires which he displaces onto
the object of his idealized passion. Just as Don Pedro indulges Beatrice
and Benedick in a fiction which corresponds to his own secret wishes,
so his brother Don John indulges Claudio in a vision of his ambiguous
desires: a lustful Hero whose sexuality both attracts and repels. The
vehemence of Claudio's public slander, his "public accusation" as
Beatrice condemningly calls it, testifies to that same excess of passion
which made him idealize his beloved. Claudio has no sense of human
weakness and therefore responds with selfish cruelty to the disappointment of his imagination. His world is an imaginative construct which
has encompassed reality by halves—only its romance and none of its
frail humanity. His sense of self is so dependent on his imagined ideal
vision of love that when that vision is disappointed, his own identity is
threatened. We in the audience are doubly aware of his lack of human
compassion because we know Hero is falsely accused. Her "sin" en-
dangers him because on some level it corresponds with his own repressed desire.

Neither the historical argument that the Elizabethans expected
such a public repudiation, nor the attempts to excuse the count's
behavior at the church on the grounds of a lofty idealism and disgust
toward sexuality, exonerate Claudio. Most readers agree with Chambers that "Claudio stands revealed as the worm that he is." His
rejection of Hero is somewhat roundabout, a combination, it would
seem, of his own desire for a shocking revelation and the bystanders',
particularly Leonato's ignorance. Shakespeare casts the opening interchange into the "plain form of marriage" so that Claudio seems to
comply with a code even in his repudiation. When the friar asks if he
comes "to marry this lady," the count says no, but he is interpreted by
Leonato to be quibbling over the way in which Friar Francis poses the
question. Claudio lets this interpretation stand. After another such
exchange, he takes over from the friar and proceeds with the ritual
forms himself, but his questions are as misleading as his earlier responses. His ambiguous question at 4.1.26–27, with its ironic reference to Hero as "this rich and precious gift," and Pedro's similarly
deceptive response, allow Leonato once again to misinterpret his inten-

tions. Finally, Claudio openly repudiates his bride, but his compliance with the ritual forms of the ceremonial occasion confirms our sense of the count's character as bounded by conventional codes.

Having returned Hero to her father, Claudio's anger and passion break forth. The emphasis shifts from the ceremonial occasion and its ordained participants—priest, father, bride and groom—to Hero herself. The demonstratives ("*this* rotten orange, *that* blood, *these* exterior shows") and the appeals to the audience ("Behold," "all you that see her") bespeak the count's determination to achieve an effect. Again Leonato misinterprets Claudio's words, for he believes the young man himself to have "made defeat of her virginity." Claudio's claim of bashful sincerity and comely love brings Hero's innocent but unfortunate reference to "seeming," which prompts his passionate denunciation. Critics have noted the similarity between Claudio's language here and that of Hamlet and Othello:

> Out on thee, seeming! I will write against it.
> You seem to me as Dian in her orb,
> As chaste as is the bud ere it be blown;
> But you are more intemperate in your blood
> Than Venus, or those pamper'd animals
> That rage in savage sensuality.
>
> (4.1.56–61)

Claudio focuses in these lines on Hero rather than the assembled audience, a change which makes his feelings seem more intensely personal and less determined by forms and codes. Shakespeare uses the rhetoric of consciousness to endow Claudio with an inner life that breaks the confines of literary convention and ceremonial decorum. Instead of the courtly lover of the previous action, he becomes an individual of psychological complexity whom we both pity and despise. His description of Hero is based on the paradoxical contrast between what she seems and what he knows she is: "Her blush is guiltiness, not modesty" (4.1.41). The irony is that the opposite is true, for what "seems," is, and what he "knows," is false. As in earlier speeches in which we find such rhetoric creating an inner self, paradox and antithesis represent Claudio's divided mind. Though addressed to Leonato, the series of questions beginning at line 69 are rhetorical and establish the pronominal contrast between "I" and "you." They also situate Claudio firmly in the moment and the real world, a necessary feature of dialogue. The count makes of Hero two persons, a Diana and a Venus, "most foul, most fair" (l. 103), and this divided Hero represents in language the poles of his own divided self. His lament, "O Hero! What a Hero hadst thou been" betrays genuine emotion. Here he is oblivious to family and friends, preoccupied with feelings, not forms. From an excess of idealism in love, Claudio is transformed into a suspicious misogynist who knows himself no better than before. Until he learns how he has been deceived, he cannot know himself, recognize his failures, and love properly.

Friar Francis restores sanity and reason to the impassioned scene of denunciation by recognizing Hero's honesty and by proposing still another "suppose," her feigned death. He argues the fundamental comic perspective of losing to find:

> for it so falls out
> That what we have we prize not to the worth
> Whiles we enjoy it, but being lack'd and lost,
> Why then we rack the value, then we find
> The virtue that possession would not show us
> Whiles it was ours: so will it fare with Claudio
> When he shall hear she died upon his words,
> Th'idea of her life shall sweetly creep
> Into his study of imagination,
> And every lovely organ of her life
> Shall come apparell'd in more precious habit,
> More moving-delicate and full of life,
> Into the eye and prospect of his soul
> Than when she liv'd indeed: then shall he mourn—
>
> (4.1.217–30)

The friar understands that Claudio has loved the idea of Hero; when the count learns of his mistake, he says "Sweet Hero! Now thy *image* doth appear / In the rare semblance that I lov'd it first" (5.1.245–46, emphasis added). Friar Francis expects to transform Claudio's imagination and lead him to a more just judgment of Hero, but the "idea of her life" never has time to "sweetly creep / Into his study of imagination."

Immediately following the scene in which Claudio learns of Hero's death, Benedick gives his challenge. Critics have been disturbed by the jesting in this scene, but Claudio's callousness would not claim our attention had Shakespeare not set up expectations for his development which are never met. Friar Francis's prediction that the count will mourn Hero "though he thought his accusation true" leads us to expect a repentance like Flamminio's in *Gl'Ingannati* where Lelia's beloved condemns his past behavior even before he learns of her love and loyalty. Even more important, our sense of Claudio's inner life, of his passionate disappointment, genuine emotion and divided mind, leads us to expect a different, more feeling response to the news of Hero's death. Though there are sound theatrical reasons for delaying Claudio's response to the more dramatic moment of confrontation with Leonato after Borachio has confessed the crime, the count's heartlessness is troubling because it fails to fulfill our expectations for the comic plot.

If we compare Shakespeare's presentation of Claudio with that of Beatrice and Benedick, we can see how he extends the convention of mistaken identity to add depth and interest to their characters, but without transgressing the carefully defined limits of their comic plot. In Benedick's soliloquy in 2.3, immediately preceding the eavesdropping scene, Shakespeare presents a character already aware of love's transforming potential. Speculating on Claudio's transformation, Benedick remembers how his friend had once "no music with him but the drum and the fife, and now had he rather hear the tabor and the pipe" (ll. 13–15). He questions his own identity, wondering whether he may, "be so converted and see with these eyes?" "Yet I am well," he repeats, trying to convince himself. The modal verbs he uses are *shall* and *will*, not *should* and *would*, future rather than subjunctive; his language betrays his openness to loving Beatrice.

Pedro, Leonato and Claudio present Benedick with the strong evidence of Beatrice's attachment he needs to admit his love. The deceivers spend very little time talking of Benedick's scorn. Instead, they recount the signs of Beatrice's love: she is up twenty times a night to write to him, beats her heart and tears her hair. Hero even fears she may do herself harm. They wish Benedick "would modestly examine himself, to see how much he is unworthy so good a lady" (2.3.200–201). And that is exactly what he does. The ease with which Benedick is "converted," or in the language of the play, "caught," makes it clear how close to the surface his love has been: "Love me? Why, it must be requited" (ll. 215–16). In his previous soliloquy he asks "can I be so converted"; here he has been converted indeed. Benedick is willing to change: "Happy are they that hear their detractions and can put them to mending." His vision altered by knowledge of Beatrice's love, Benedick now begins to interpret her differently. What was once judged quarrelsome is now thought loving. His notion of himself and of her has changed, and consequently her words have different meanings.

Despite this change, his character still conforms to the broad outlines of a comic stereotype, the *miles gloriosus*. His boasting of success with women and his martial reputation connect him to the *miles* tradition just as Claudio's language and actions have connected him to the tradition of the courtly lover. After the slander of Hero, when he and Beatrice admit their love, Benedick's avowals imply his martial talents: "By my sword, Beatrice, thou lovest me," (4.1.272) and "I will swear by it that you love me, and I will make him eat it that says I love not you." But unlike the Plautine braggart, Benedick is truly a martial hero and his engagement to Beatrice to fight Claudio is real. In Benedick Shakespeare has created an individual character who is also a comic type, a talent for which we should remember Donatus and other commentators praise Terence.

The deceit of Beatrice presents a very different fiction. Hero and Margaret emphasize not Benedick's love, but Beatrice's disdain. They exaggerate her scorn for the opposite sex, describe her derision of a man's love and compliment Benedick's worth and valor. Their fable portrays a Beatrice whose wit protects her from emotional involvement. The deceits perpetrated by the other characters satisfy the individual needs of each other: Benedick's fragile ego needs the safety of Beatrice's love in order to admit his own; Beatrice's fear of male domination makes her scorn love. Her soliloquy, like Benedick's, is filled with rhetorical questions, paradox, and the juxtaposition of past, present and future, all features of dialogue. But there are significant differences in the two lovers' speeches. Beatrice speaks in verse, and the shift to poetry, the first she uses in the play, marks the liberation of her desire. Whereas Benedick wonders whether he can change and love Beatrice, she questions whether or not he loves her. Their individual responses bear out the differences in the way they are gulled: Benedick through his self-love; Beatrice through her "wild heart" which makes her fear domination by men.

Even with these visions of the other's affections, however, it takes the heightened emotion of the church scene, an impossible moment for their usual self-protective repartee, for Beatrice and Benedick to let down their defenses and admit their mutual love. When Leonato tells them they were "lent eyes to see," he telescopes the way in which the play juxtaposes mistaken identity with mistaken insight. Mistaken identity, role-playing and alternate identities are therapeutic instruments which lead the characters to self-knowledge, for these comic devices are not simply tools for developing plot, but springboards for experimentation whereby men and women escape from self-delusion to the self-understanding which enables them to live and love.

Comic decorum, which dictates the lovers' conversion to love, also prohibits Claudio's being made into a tragic figure who undergoes a psychologically "real" development. He cannot, argues M. C. Bradbrook, be "allowed more than a pretty lyric by way of remorse." Critics have claimed that Claudio's behaviour can best be understood within the context of a Decameron-like story, but as we have seen in 4.1, Shakespeare endows him with a psychological complexity in excess of what such a plot requires. No reading of the play can excuse the brutality of his treatment of Hero, but the conventional comic action does demand that he be forgiven. When he learns of his mistake, Claudio asks of Leonato, "Impose me to what penance your invention / Can lay upon my sin; yet sinn'd I not / But in mistaking" (5.1.267–69). But for Shakespeare, mistaking is enough; the play asserts that the sins of ignorance and credulity have consequences as dire as Don John's sins of will. Claudio's explicitly religious penance at Hero's tomb, though only sketched, is a conventional means of dramatizing his movement through sin and confession to repentance and self-knowledge. Though certainly a "pretty lyric," Claudio's lines also unite *Much Ado* with the dark comedies and late romances in their emphasis on ritual forgiveness.

Much Ado about Nothing richly deserves the frequently drawn comparison with *Measure for Measure*. Just as the intensity of Angelo's appetite for Isabella and her vehement rejection of her brother's plea to live threaten our sense that comic conventions are adequate to our experience of that play, so Claudio's repudiation of Hero in the church scene, and his untractable unwillingness to conform to Friar Francis's comic vision of losing to find, trouble our satisfaction with *Much Ado's* comic resolution.

In both *Much Ado* and *Measure for Measure*, the careful balance between the conventions of comic plotting and those of lifelike characterization which Shakespeare maintains in his earlier comedies is upset. The rhetoric of consciousness which he employs adds depth and complexity to his comic characters and to the convention of mistaken identity, extending it from a plot device to a means of representing character development on stage. This inner life receives an emphasis more characteristic of tragic than of comic drama. In the criticism of tragedy, comic intrusions were once called "comic relief," but both the pejorative term itself and its correspondingly reductive view of such scenes in tragedy have been rejected in favor of a larger claim for the tragic vision, its expansiveness and complexity. A similar prejudice has troubled the criticism of Shakespeare's comedies, and to a limited extent those of his predecessors. Too often, critics have judged his use of a deliberative mode of comic characterization as a kind of bumbling intrusion of the tragic into comedy, whether in terms of Renaissance readers and audiences such as Sidney and Johnson, who labeled such plays "mongrel tragicomedy," or modern Shakespeareans who criticize Claudio's outburst in the church scene, or the problematic generic status of *Measure for Measure*.

Angelo is, of course, more interesting and complex a poetic creation than Claudio. In part this difference can be explained in simple quantitative terms—Angelo has a much greater portion of the lines and share in the action of *Measure for Measure* than Claudio has in *Much Ado*, in which the displacement of the main plot maintains our sense that the "ado" is about "nothing." But there are more significant differences. Shakespeare's portrayal of Claudio as courtly lover is less interesting than that of Angelo as ascetic and judge. Angelo is not bound by the conventions of type character which Shakespeare found so useful in creating Claudio and making his gullibility believable. Most important, of course, is Angelo's self-consciousness, the recognition of his own shortcomings and failures which Shakespeare renders so vividly in the soliloquies in 2.2.167ff. and later in 2.4.1–30. By making Angelo self-conscious about his desire for Isabella, by having him debate its merits and consequences, Shakespeare creates a complex comic character who arrests our imaginations.

Generic complexity is a feature of Shakespeare's dramatic practice, and as Rosalie Colie has argued, of Renaissance habits of reading and writing generally. Many have remarked that the comedies and romances contain within them tragic actions; recently, Shakespeareans have identified comic matrices in the great tragedies. I have argued that the generic boundaries of characterization are as flexible in Shakespeare's dramaturgy as those of plot and structure; because he often uses deliberative strategies common to tragic characterization within the dramatic boundaries of his romantic comedies, we perceive his comic characters as complex and lifelike.

Chronology

1564   William Shakespeare born at Stratford-on-Avon to John
        Shakespeare, a butcher, and Mary Arden. He is bap-
        tized on April 26.

1582   Marries Anne Hathaway in November.

1583   Daughter Susanna born, baptized on May 26.

1585   Twins Hamnet and Judith born, baptized on Febru-
        ary 2.

1588–90 Sometime during these years, Shakespeare goes to Lon-
        don, without family. First plays performed in London.

1590–92 *The Comedy of Errors*, the three parts of *Henry VI*.

1593–94 Publication of *Venus and Adonis* and *The Rape of Lucrece*,
        both dedicated to the earl of Southampton. Shake-
        speare becomes a sharer in the Lord Chamberlain's com-
        pany of actors. *The Taming of the Shrew, The Two
        Gentlemen of Verona, Richard III, Titus Andronicus.*

1595–97 *Romeo and Juliet, Richard II, King John, A Midsummer
        Night's Dream, Love's Labor's Lost.*

1596   Son Hamnet dies. Grant of arms to Shakespeare's father.

1597   *The Merchant of Venice, Henry IV, Part 1.* Purchases
        New Place in Stratford.

1598–1600 *Henry IV, Part 2, As You Like It, Much Ado about Noth-
        ing, Twelfth Night, The Merry Wives of Windsor, Henry
        V,* and *Julius Caesar.* Moves his company to the new
        Globe Theatre.

1601   *Hamlet.* Shakespeare's father dies, buried on September 8.

1601–2 *Troilus and Cressida.*

1603   Death of Queen Elizabeth; James VI of Scotland be-
        comes James I of England; Shakespeare's company be-
        comes the King's Men.

1603–4	*All's Well That Ends Well, Measure for Measure, Othello.*
1605–6	*King Lear, Macbeth.*
1607	Marriage of daughter Susanna on June 5.
1607–8	*Timon of Athens, Antony and Cleopatra, Pericles, Coriolanus.*
1608	Shakespeare's mother dies, buried on September 9.
1609	*Cymbeline,* publication of sonnets. Shakespeare's company purchases Blackfriars Theatre.
1610–11	*The Winter's Tale, The Tempest.* Shakespeare retires to Stratford.
1612–13	*Henry VIII, The Two Noble Kinsmen.*
1616	Marriage of daughter Judith on February 10. Shakespeare dies at Stratford on April 23.
1623	Publication of the Folio edition of Shakespeare's plays.

Contributors

HAROLD BLOOM, Sterling Professor of the Humanities at Yale University, is the author of *The Anxiety of Influence, Poetry and Repression,* and many other volumes of literary criticism. His forthcoming study, *Freud: Transference and Authority,* attempts a full-scale reading of all of Freud's major writings. A MacArthur Prize Fellow, he is general editor of five series of literary criticism published by Chelsea House. During 1987–88, he served as Charles Eliot Norton Professor of Poetry at Harvard University.

RUTH NEVO is Professor of English at Hebrew University in Jerusalem. She is the author of *Comic Transformations in Shakespeare, Tragic Form in Shakespeare,* and numerous other works. She has also translated into English the *Selected Poems* of Chaim Nachman Bialik.

HARRY BERGER, JR., is Professor of English at the University of California, Santa Cruz. His works include *The Allegorical Temper* and numerous articles on Shakespeare, Spenser, Milton, and Robert Frost.

JOHN TRAUGOTT, Professor of English at the University of California, Berkeley, is the author of numerous books and articles on sixteenth-, seventeenth-, and eighteenth-century comic literature.

JOSEPH WESTLUND is Associate Professor of English at Northeastern University, Boston. He is the author of *Shakespeare's Reparative Comedy: A Psychoanalytic View of the Middle Plays.*

RICHARD A. LEVIN, Associate Professor of English at the University of California, Davis, is the author of *Love and Society in Shakespearean Comedy: A Study of Dramatic Form and Content.*

CAROL THOMAS NEELY teaches English at Illinois State University.

She is coeditor of *The Woman's Part: Feminist Criticism of Shakespeare* and the author of *Broken Nuptials in Shakespeare's Plays*.

KAREN NEWMAN is Assistant Professor of Comparative Literature at Brown University and the author of *Shakespeare's Rhetoric of Comic Character*.

Bibliography

Barber, C. L. *Shakespeare's Festive Comedy: A Study of Dramatic Form and Its Relation to Social Custom*. Princeton: Princeton University Press, 1959.

Barish, Jonas A. "Pattern and Purpose in the Prose of *Much Ado about Nothing*." *Rice University Studies* 60 (1974): 20–28.

Berry, Ralph. *Shakespeare's Comedies: Explorations in Form*. Princeton: Princeton University Press, 1972.

Bradbrook, M. C. *The Growth and Structure of Elizabethan Comedy*. London: Chatto & Windus, 1955.

Brown, John Russell. *Shakespeare and His Comedies*. 2d ed. London: Methuen, 1962.

Bullough, Geoffrey, ed. *Narrative and Dramatic Sources of Shakespeare*. Vol. 2, *The Comedies, 1597–1603*. New York: Columbia University Press, 1968.

Burckhardt, Sigurd. *Shakespearean Meanings*. Princeton: Princeton University Press, 1968.

Champion, Larry. *The Evolution of Shakespeare's Comedy: A Study in Dramatic Perspective*. Cambridge: Harvard University Press, 1970.

Coghill, Nevill. "The Basis of Shakespearean Comedy." In *Shakespeare Criticism: 1935–1960*, edited by Anne Ridler. Oxford: Oxford University Press, 1970.

Dawson, Anthony B. "Much Ado about Signifying." *Studies in English Literature 1500–1900* 22 (1982: 212–21.

Elam, Keir. *Shakespeare's Universe of Discourse: Language-Games in the Comedies*. Cambridge: Cambridge University Press, 1984.

Evans, Bertrand. *Shakespeare's Comedies*. Oxford: Clarendon Press, 1960.

Everett, Barbara. "*Much Ado about Nothing*." *Critical Quarterly* 3 (1961): 319–33.

Felperin, Howard. *Shakespearean Romance*. Princeton: Princeton University Press, 1972.

Frye, Northrop. "The Argument of Comedy." In *English Institute Essays*, edited by D. A. Robertson, Jr., 58–73. New York: Columbia University Press, 1949.

———. *A Natural Perspective: The Development of Shakespearean Comedy and Romance*. New York: Columbia University Press, 1965.

———. *The Secular Scripture: A Study of the Structure of Romance*. Cambridge: Harvard University Press, 1976.

Goddard, Harold C. *The Meaning of Shakespeare*. Chicago: University of Chicago Press, 1951.

Hays, Janice. " 'Those Soft and Delicate Desires': *Much Ado* and the Distrust of Women." In *The Woman's Part: Feminist Criticism of Shakespeare*, edited by Carolyn Ruth Swift Lenz, Gayle Greene, and Carol Thomas Neely. Urbana: University of Illinois Press, 1980.

Hunter, G. K. *Shakespeare: The Later Comedies*. London: Longmans, 1962.

Hunter, Robert Grams. *Shakespeare and the Comedy of Forgiveness*. New York: Columbia University Press, 1965.

Huston, J. Dennis. *Shakespeare's Comedies of Play*. New York: Columbia University Press, 1981.

Kirsch, Arthur. *Shakespeare and the Experience of Love*. Cambridge: Harvard University Press, 1981.

Krieger, Elliot. *A Marxist Study of Shakespeare's Comedies*. London: Macmillan, 1979.

———. "Social Relations and the Social Order in *Much Ado about Nothing*." *Shakespeare Survey* 32 (1979): 49–61.

Leggatt, Alexander. *Shakespeare's Comedy of Love*. London, Methuen, 1974.

MacCary, W. Thomas. *Friends and Lovers: The Phenomenology of Desire in Shakespearian Comedy*. New York: Columbia University Press, 1985.

Martz, William J. *Shakespeare's Universe of Comedy*. New York: David Lewis, 1971.

Muir, Kenneth. *Shakespeare's Comic Sequence*. Liverpool: Liverpool University Press, 1979.

Nelson, Thomas Allen. *Shakespeare's Comic Theory: A Study of Art and Artifice in the Last Plays*. The Hague: Mouton, 1972.

Ornstein, Robert. *Shakespeare's Comedies: From Roman Farce to Romantic Mystery*. Newark: University of Delaware Press, 1986.

Prouty, Charles T. *The Sources of* Much Ado about Nothing. New Haven: Yale University Press, 1950.

Riemer, A. P. *Antic Fables: Patterns of Evasion in Shakespeare's Comedies*. New York: St. Martin's, 1980.

Rossiter, A. P. *Angel with Horns and Other Shakespeare Lectures,* edited by Graham Storey. London: Longmans, 1961.

Salingar, Leo. *Shakespeare and the Traditions of Comedy*. Cambridge: Cambridge University Press, 1974.

Scott, William O. *The God of Arts: Ruling Ideas in Shakespeare's Comedies*. Lawrence: University of Kansas Publications, 1977.

Sexton, Joyce Hengerer. "The Theme of Slander in *Much Ado about Nothing* and Garter's *Susanna*." *Philological Quarterly* 54 (1975): 419–33.

Swinden, Patrick. *An Introduction to Shakespeare's Comedies*. London: Macmillan, 1973.

Williamson, Marilyn L. *The Patriarchy of Shakespeare's Comedies*. Detroit: Wayne State University Press, 1986.

Yates, Frances A. *Shakespeare's Last Plays: A New Approach*. London: Routledge & Kegan Paul, 1975.

Acknowledgments

" 'Better Than Reportingly' " by Ruth Nevo from *Comic Transformations in Shakespeare* by Ruth Nevo, © 1980 by Ruth Nevo. Reprinted by permission of Methuen & Co.

"Against the Sink-a-pace: Sexual and Family Politics in *Much Ado about Nothing*" by Harry Berger, Jr., from *Shakespeare Quarterly* 33, no. 3 (Autumn 1982), © 1982 by The Folger Shakespeare Library. Reprinted by permission.

"Creating a Rational Rinaldo: A Study in the Mixture of the Genres of Comedy and Romance in *Much Ado about Nothing*" by John Traugott from *Genre* 15, nos. 2 & 3 (Spring/Summer 1982), © 1982 by the University of Oklahoma. Reprinted by permission.

"*Much Ado about Nothing*: The Temptation to Isolate" by Joseph Westlund from *Shakespeare's Reparative Comedies: A Psychoanalytic View of the Middle Plays* by Joseph Westlund, © 1984 by the University of Chicago. Reprinted by permission of the University of Chicago Press.

"Crime and Cover-up in Messina" by Richard A. Levin from *Love and Society in Shakespearean Comedy: A Study of Dramatic Form and Content* by Richard A. Levin, © 1985 by Associated University Presses, Inc. Reprinted by permission of Associated University Presses, Inc.

"Broken Nuptials in Shakespeare's Comedies: *Much Ado about Nothing*" by Carol Thomas Neely from *Broken Nuptials in Shakespeare's Plays* by Carol Thomas Neely, © 1985 by Yale University. Reprinted by permission of Yale University Press.

"Mistaking in *Much Ado*" by Karen Newman from *Shakespeare's Rhetoric of Comic Character: Dramatic Convention in Classical and Renaissance Comedy* by Karen Newman, © 1985 by Karen Newman. Reprinted by permission of Methuen & Co.

Index

141